transfer of grace

IMAGES OF THE LOWCOUNTRY

PHOTOGRAPHS BY gary geboy

NARRATIVE BY teresa bruce

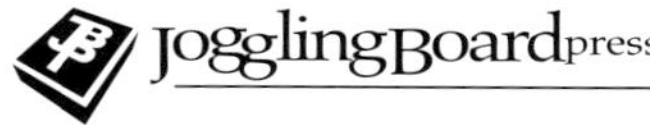

Joggling Board Press Charleston, South Carolina

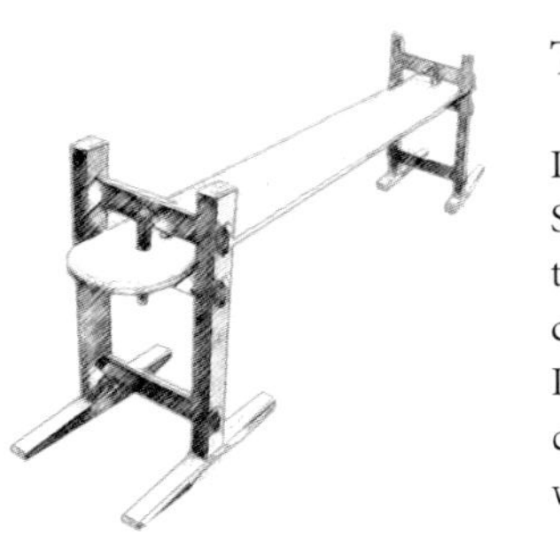

THE JOGGLING BOARD

Legend has it that the idea for the joggling board came to South Carolina from Scotland in the early 1800s. The long board supported by rockers at each end allows two or more persons to rock together. This playful outdoor furniture became a common sight in the 19th century, gracing Southern porches, yards and piazzas. It was thought to be useful in easing rheumatism, aiding digestion and bolstering courtships. Some say that no daughter went unmarried in any antebellum house with a joggling board.

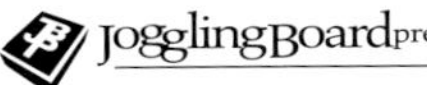

Published by Joggling Board Press
Joggling Board Press, LLC
P.O. Box 13029
Charleston, SC 29422
www.jogglingboardpress.com

First edition

Editor/publisher: Susan Kammeraad-Campbell
Associate editors: Douglas Bostick, William R. Campbell, Ph.D., Tom Smith, Ph.D.
Senior designer: Courtney Gunter

First printing 2007
Printed in Hong Kong.

A CIP catalog record for this book has been applied for from the Library of Congress.

ISBN-13: 978-0-9753498-2-3
ISBN-10: 0-9753498-2-1

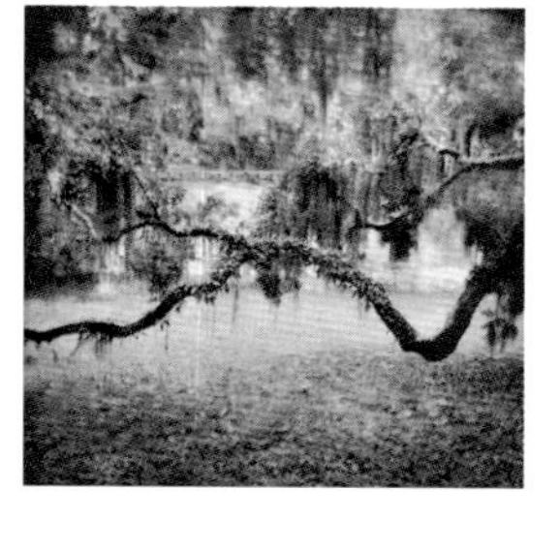

To all the live oaks, marshes, pines and herons.
I hope they survive the hand of man.

You are never alone
in the Lowcountry,
never bereft of connection.

It is impossible to hide or hoard the treasures found here. The Lowcountry always has been shared. However isolated it sometimes feels, at the end of the longest wooden dock or adrift among the shallow maze of tidal creeks, the waters are not yours alone.

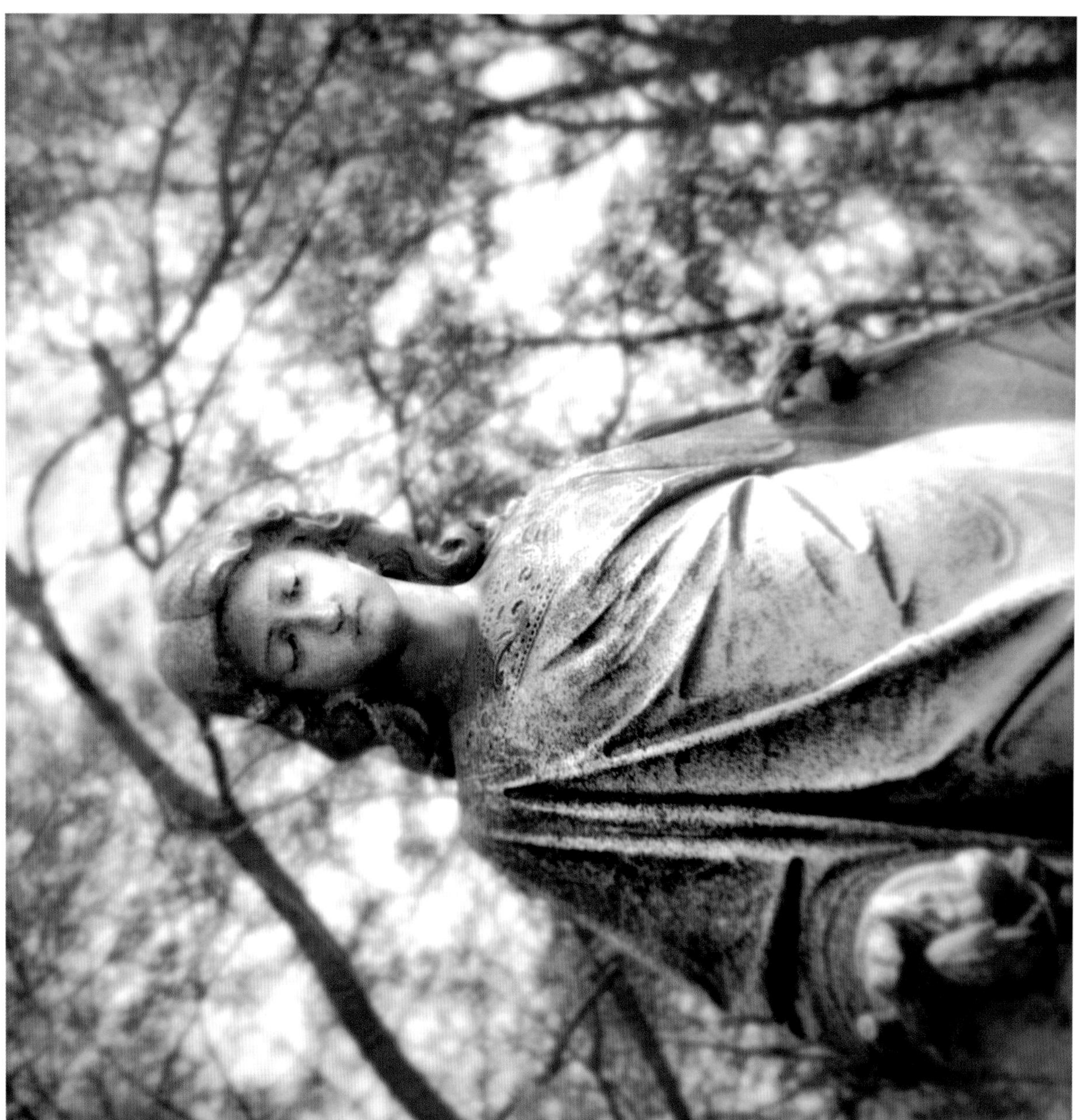

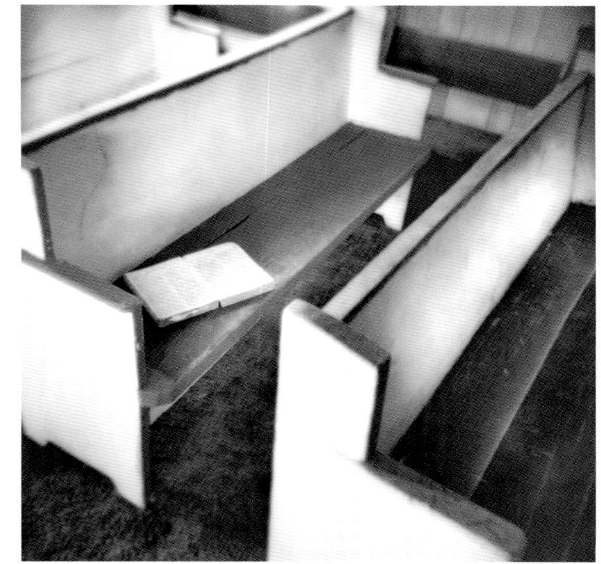

Dip under their surface and you are simply another species passing through. Untold pairs of eyes watch and react to your every move. Be still, and the sounds come to you: oysters squirting, crabs scuttling, shrimp skipping. You surface to another subtle symphony: wrens chirping, squirrels arguing, your own wake rippling through the marsh grass. It is the quiet roar of presence, continual, even if unseen.

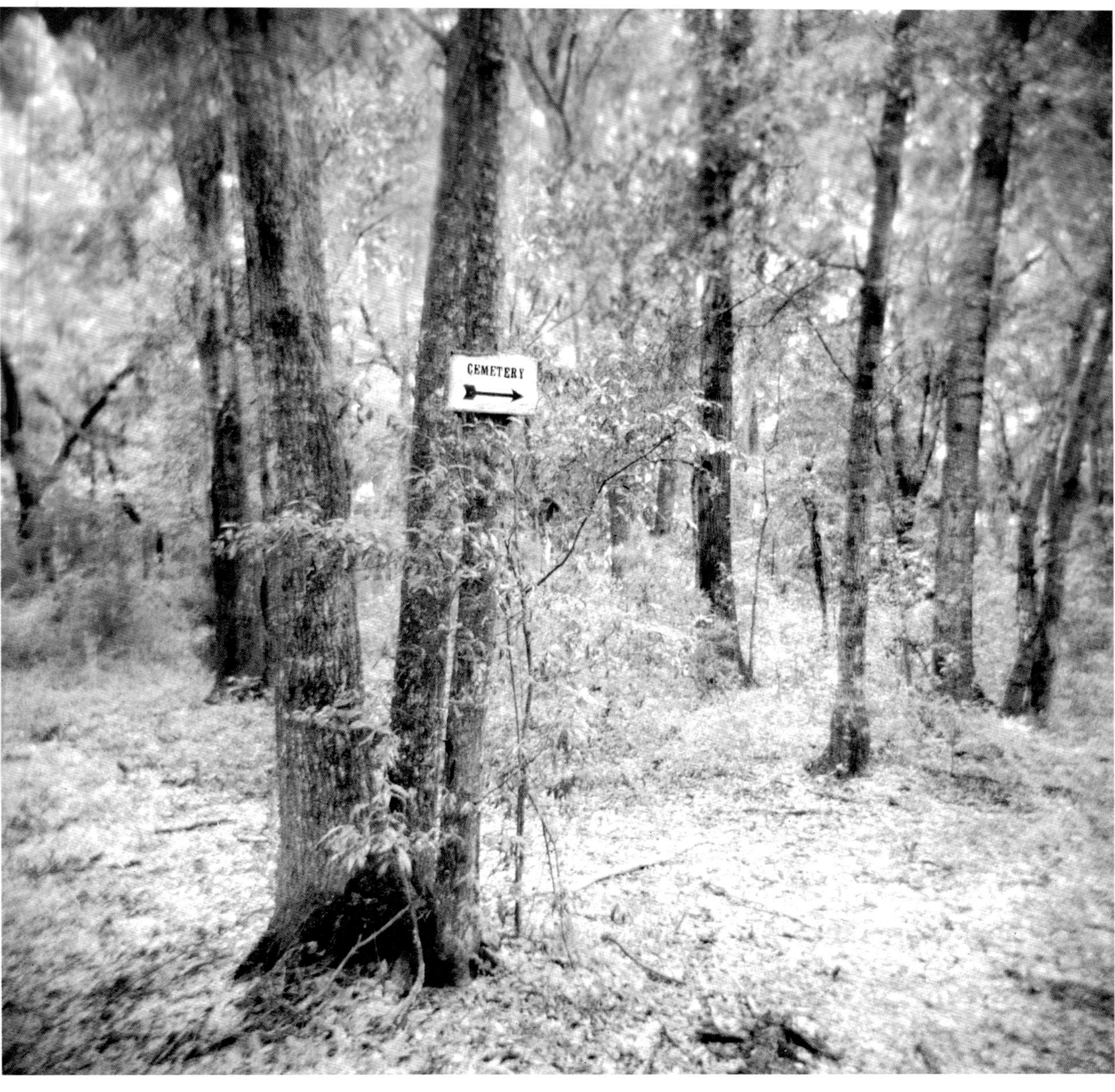
CEMETERY

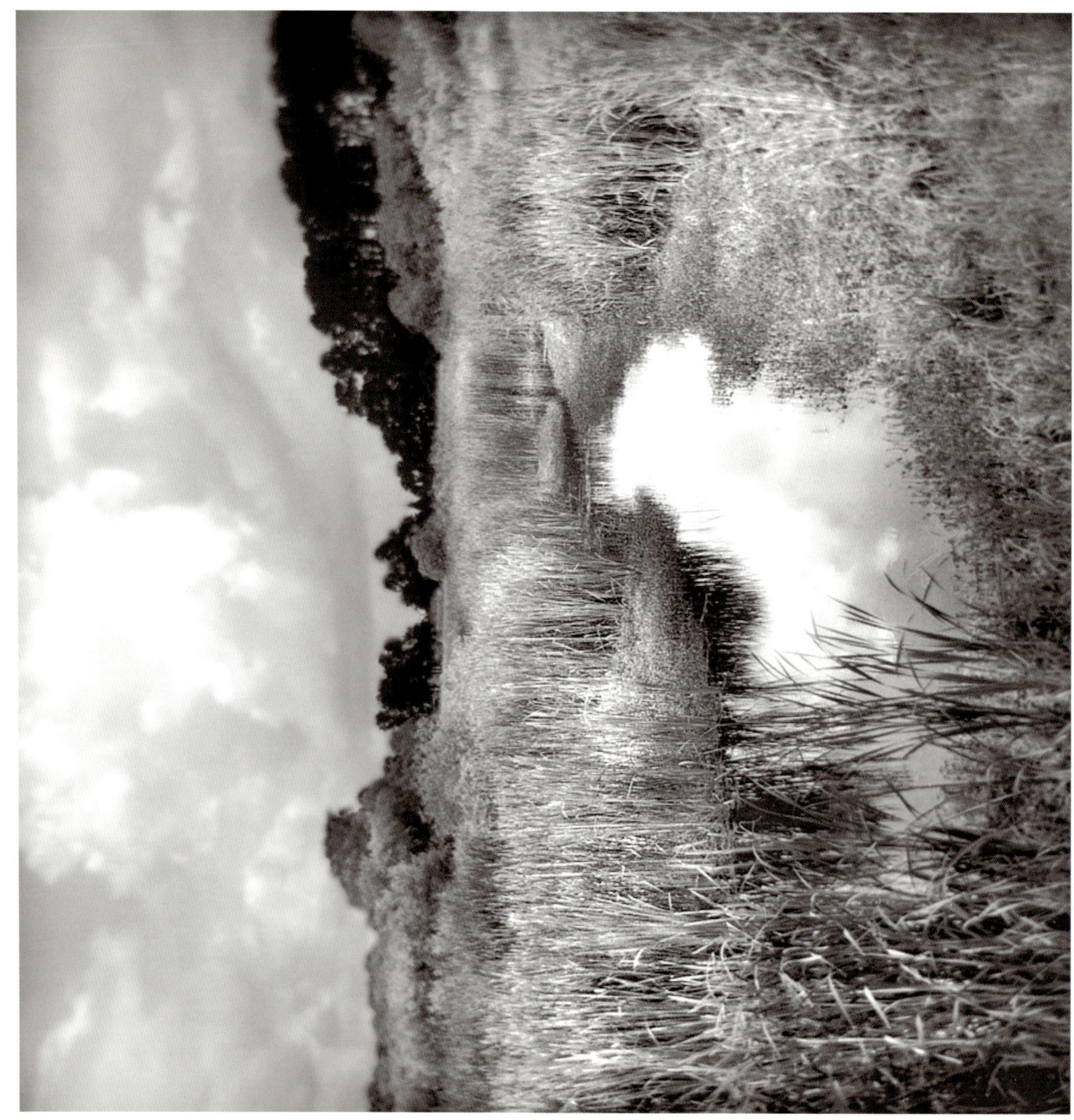

For the privilege of this connection
there is a price – addiction.

Leaving the Lowcountry is hard. Sharing, likewise, is not easy. Great is the urge to own and gate; greater is the need to step lightly. The Southeast is the last American frontier – a place apart. We are pilgrims all; searching for our past in the future, for familiarity in the unknown. Our children are grown. Our marks have been made. We want to "smell the roses" now and wander peaceful shores.

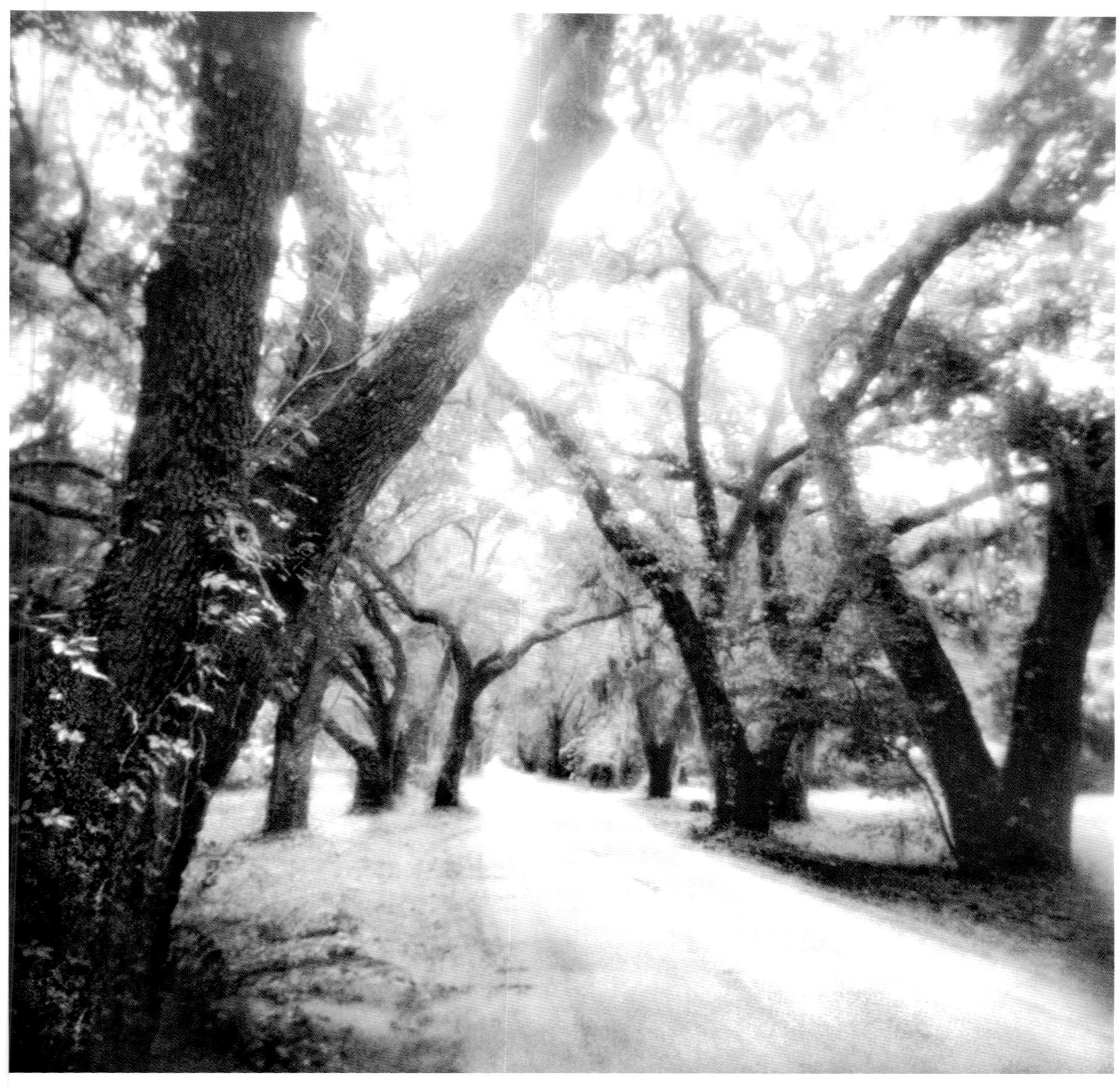

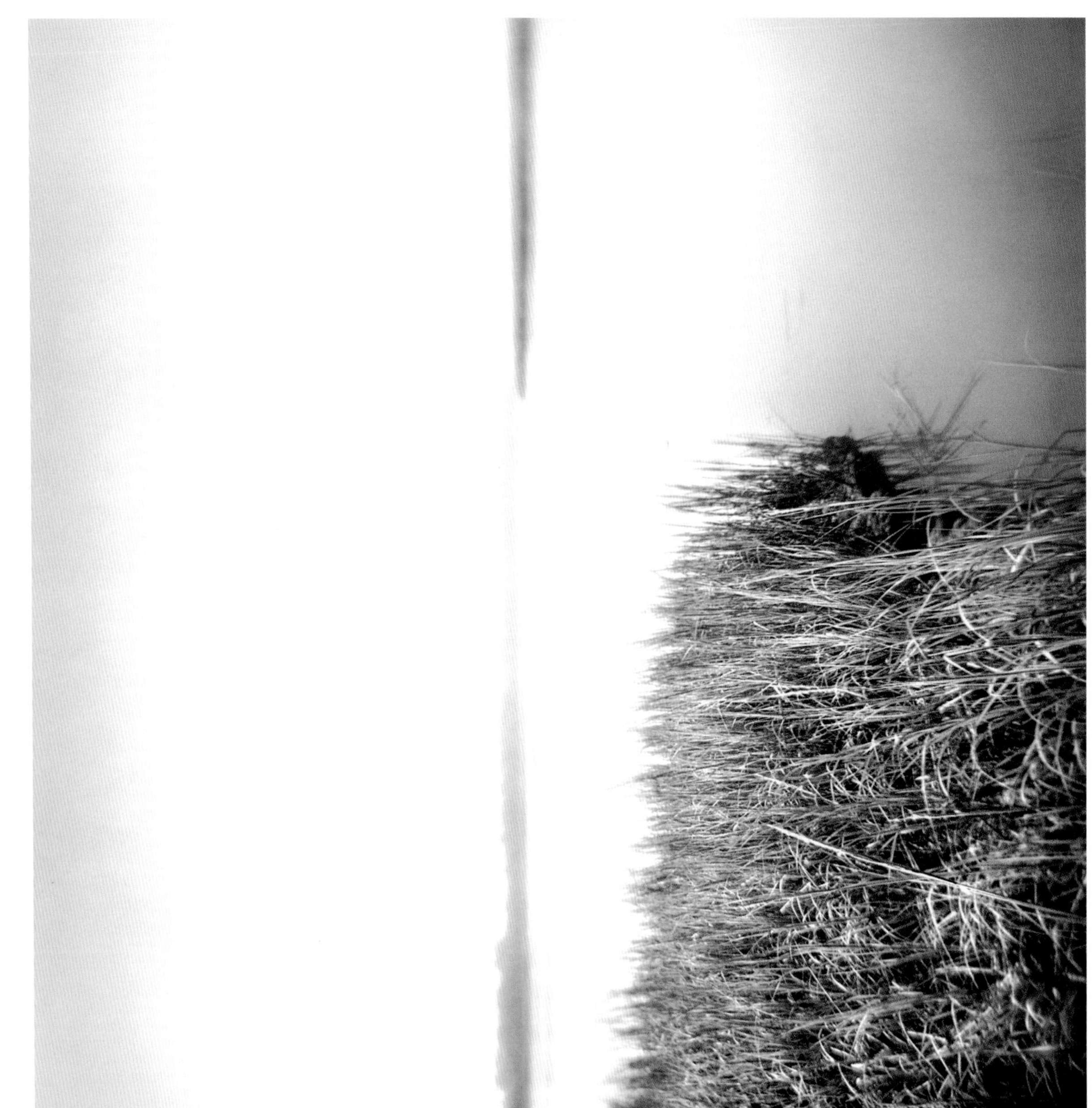

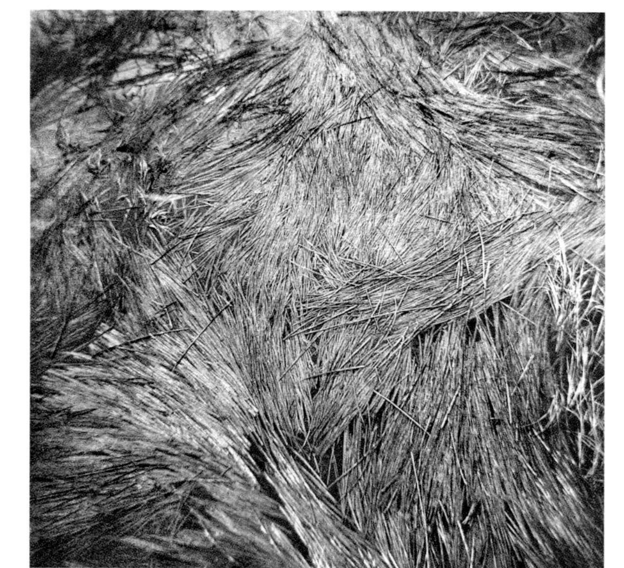

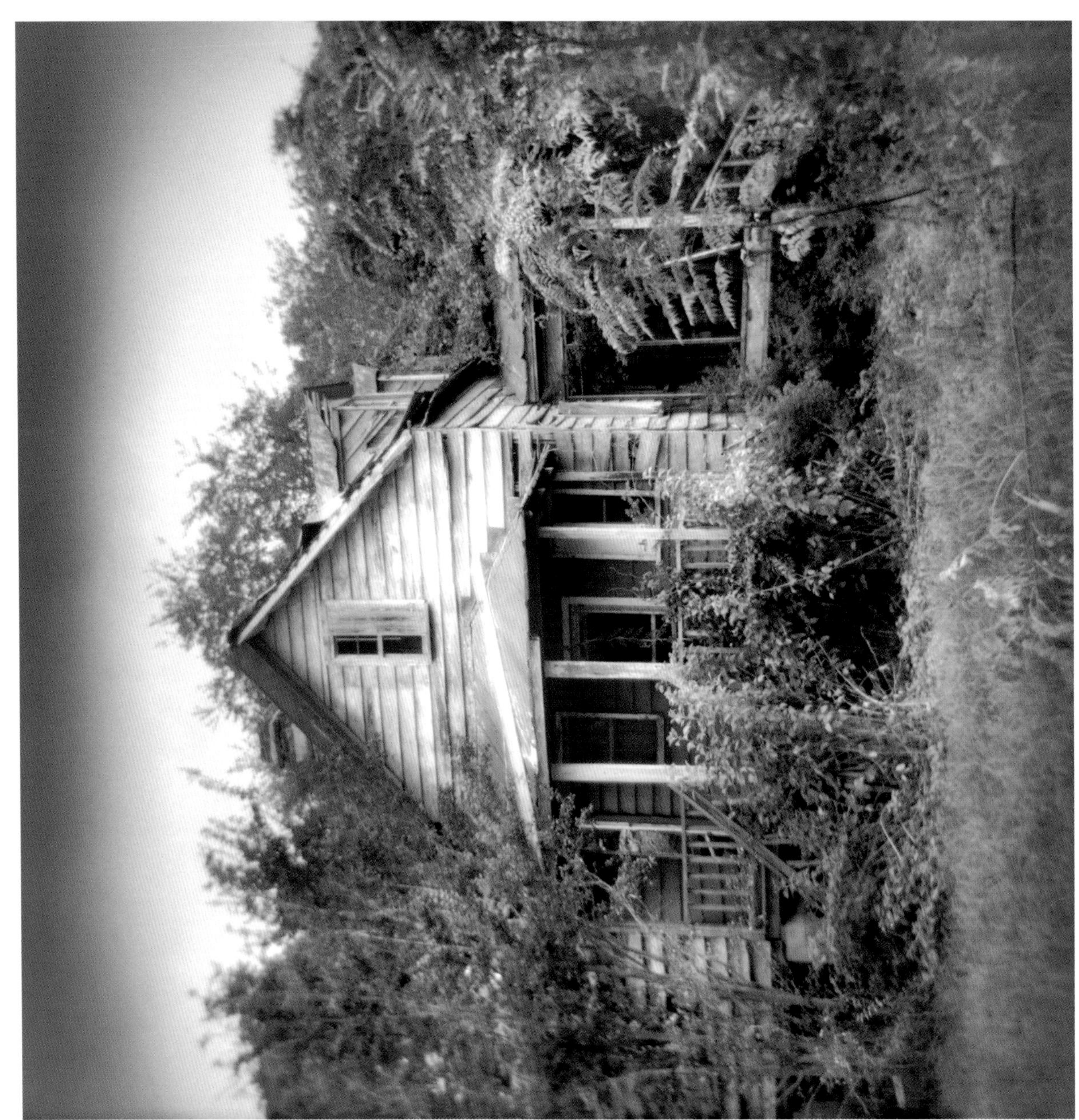

In the Lowcountry, no one really owns space. Its rivers can't be fenced. The deer and raccoons do not care where forests end and gardens begin. Alligators find outdoor swimming pools convenient oases. And every few years, nature reminds us all that we are simply guests for a time. Hurricanes take from us what we build and dare declare our own.

It’s called the Lowcountry for a reason.
Seas swell and the wind whips our
pretensions into a new order.
Our claims are rearranged.

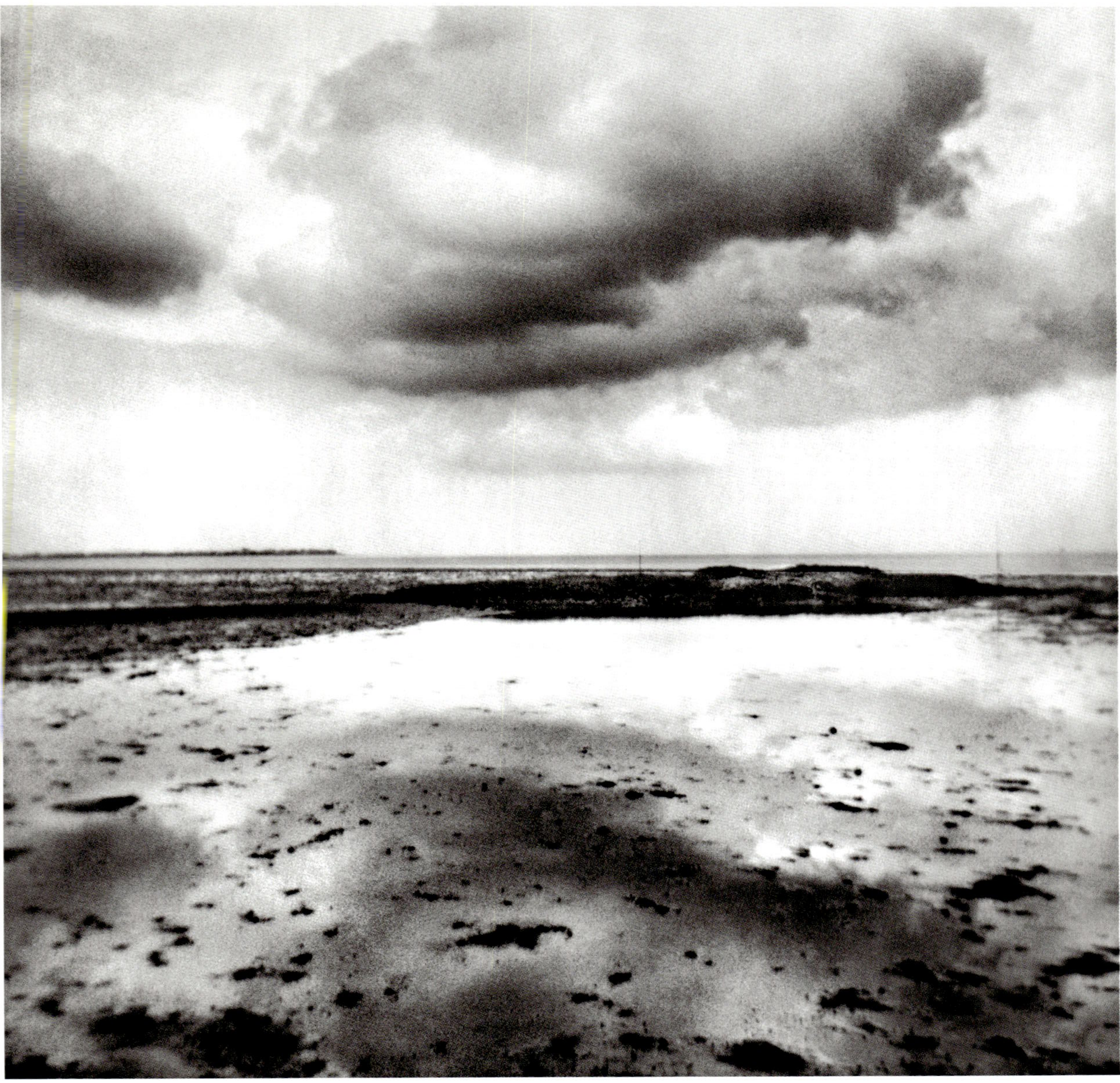

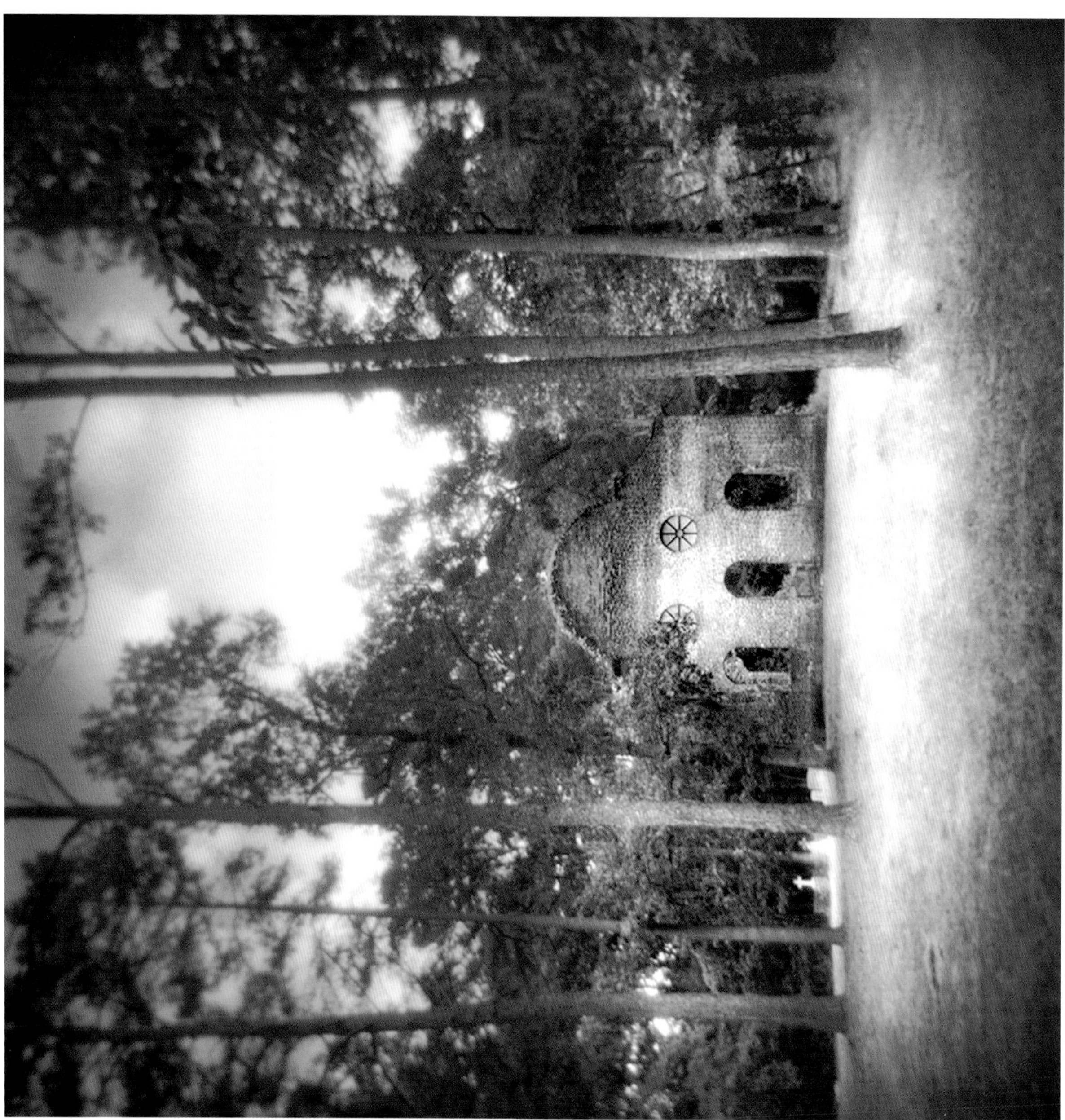

Look to the ruins of the Mayan cities of the America further south. There, the conquerors abused the earth, slashing and burning like we bulldoze and fertilize; eventually, the jungle reclaimed their temples and pyramids. Our super-sized aesthetics – golf courses and three-SUV garages – are just as vulnerable.

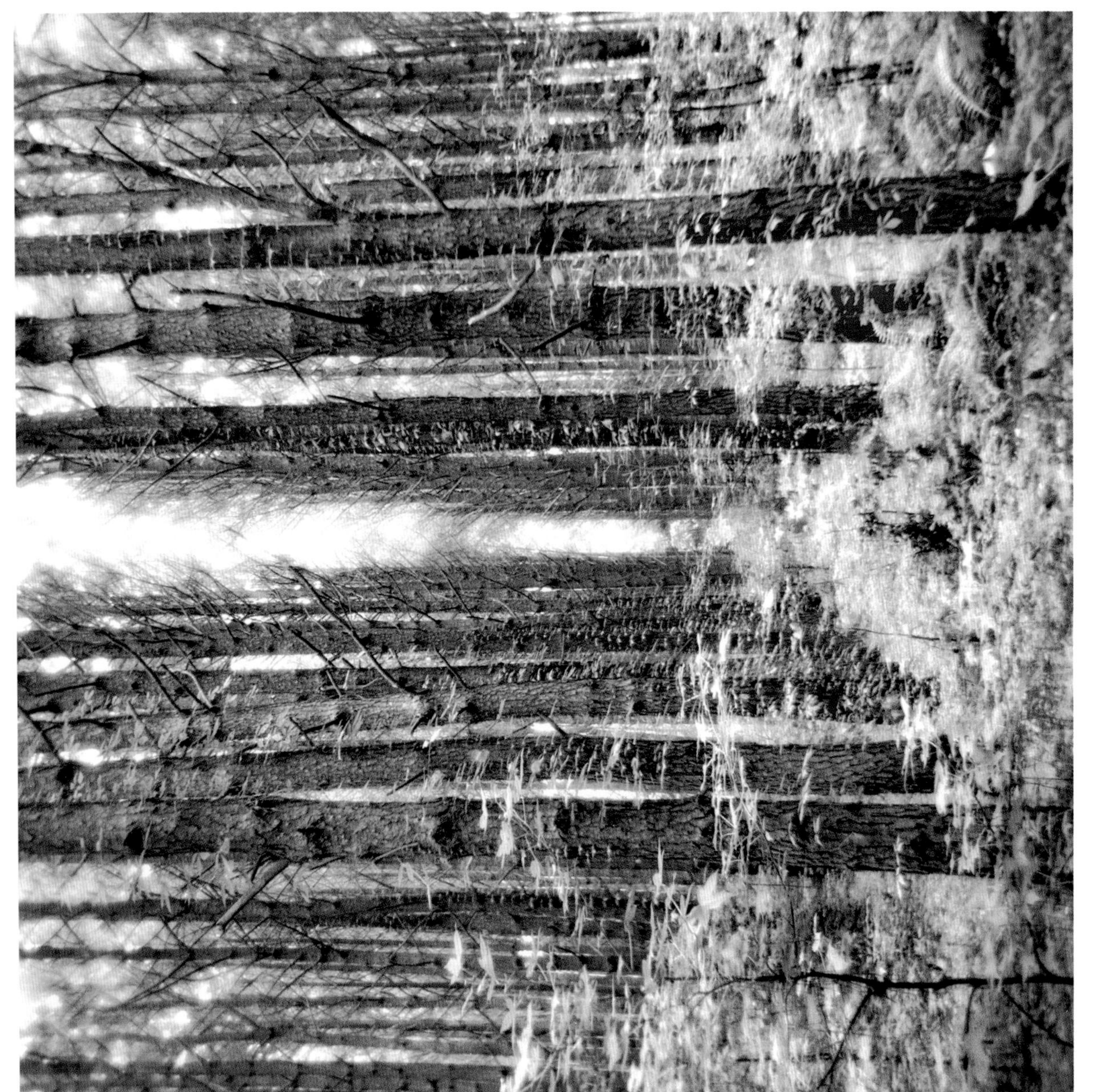

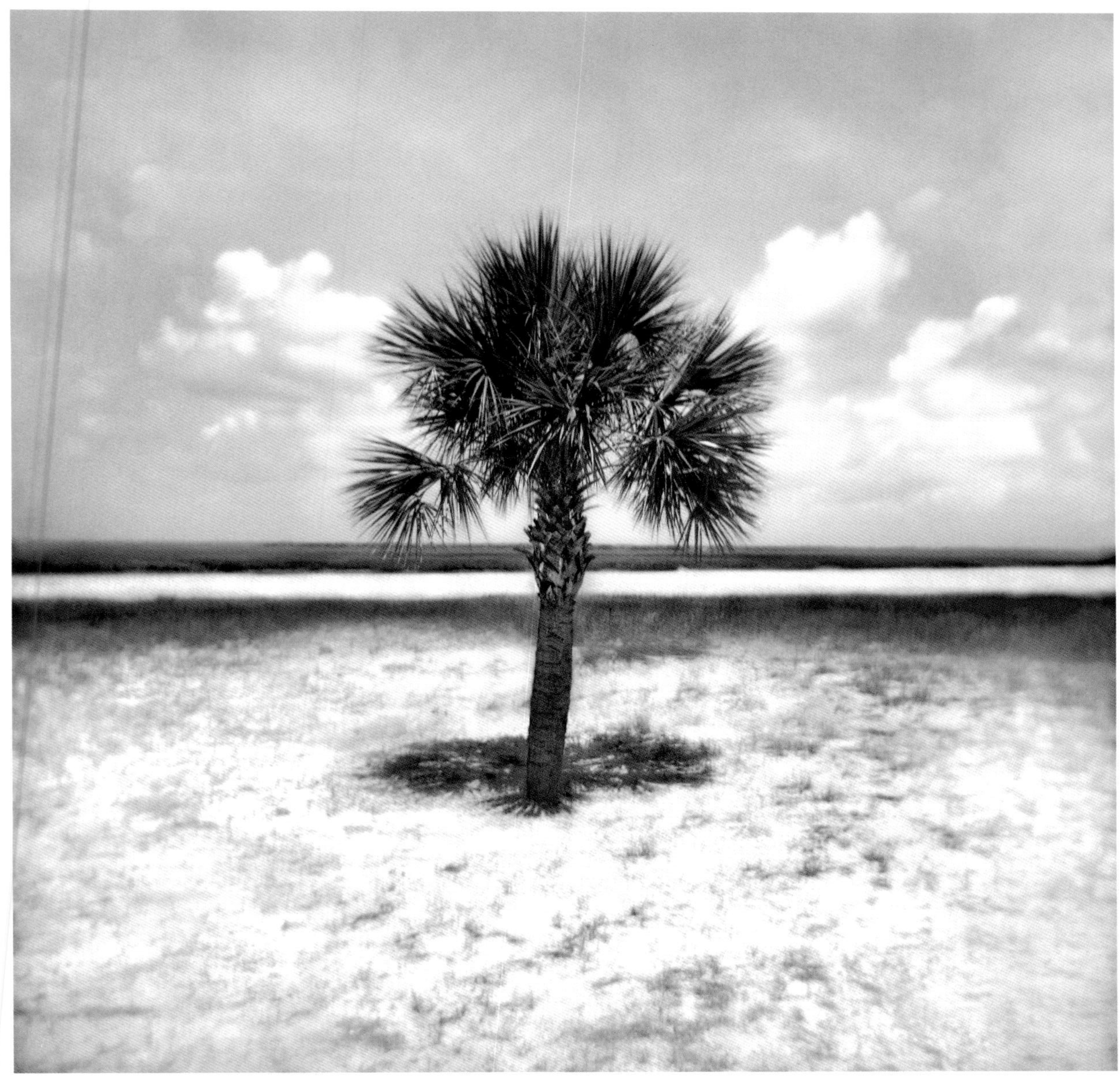

More and more of us are drawn here, away from the hassles of crowded cities. But the lure of the Lowcountry is not wilderness. Generations ago, bridges, asphalt and air conditioning ended its isolation. Pristine is not the right word either; never has been. This is a shared place, porous yet interdependent.

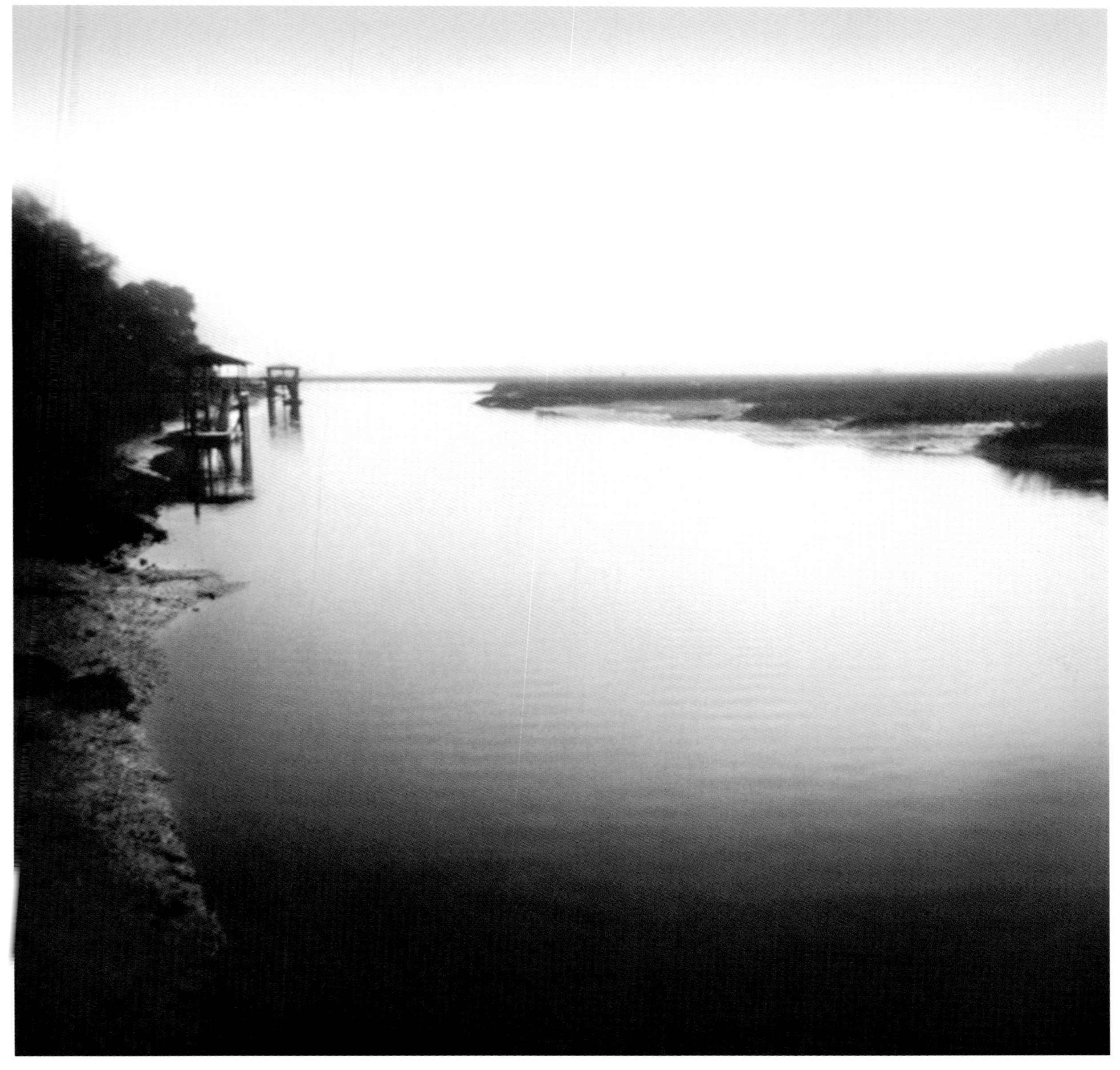

The landscape does not overwhelm;
it seduces.

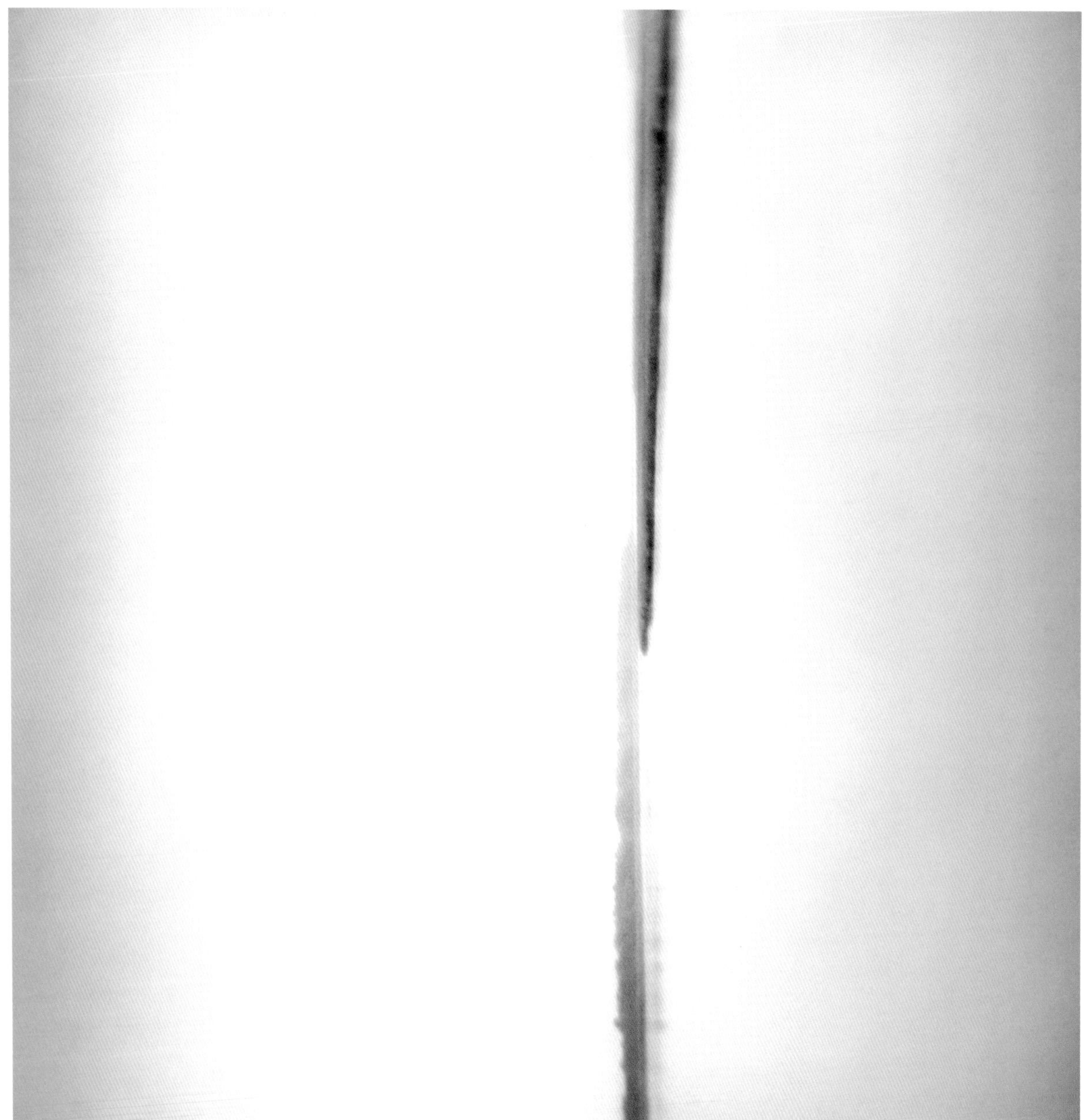

The vistas are vast, but near, and the air sweet with jasmine and sea breeze. The withering summer heat drains away our pretensions; ladies don't perspire here, they flow salty rivulets like the sun-slicked shiny cradles of low tide. Every man is an island, or at least lives on one, and hands are held out for the leap from shore to shore. Children grow up never making snowmen, and the spring is a gentle exhale rather than a thaw.

The alabaster beaches are bone yards of exposed erosion – wind-peeled trees are twisted testimony to the transitory. In the coastal forest undergrowth of saw palmetto and slash pine is the primordial tangle of splendor.

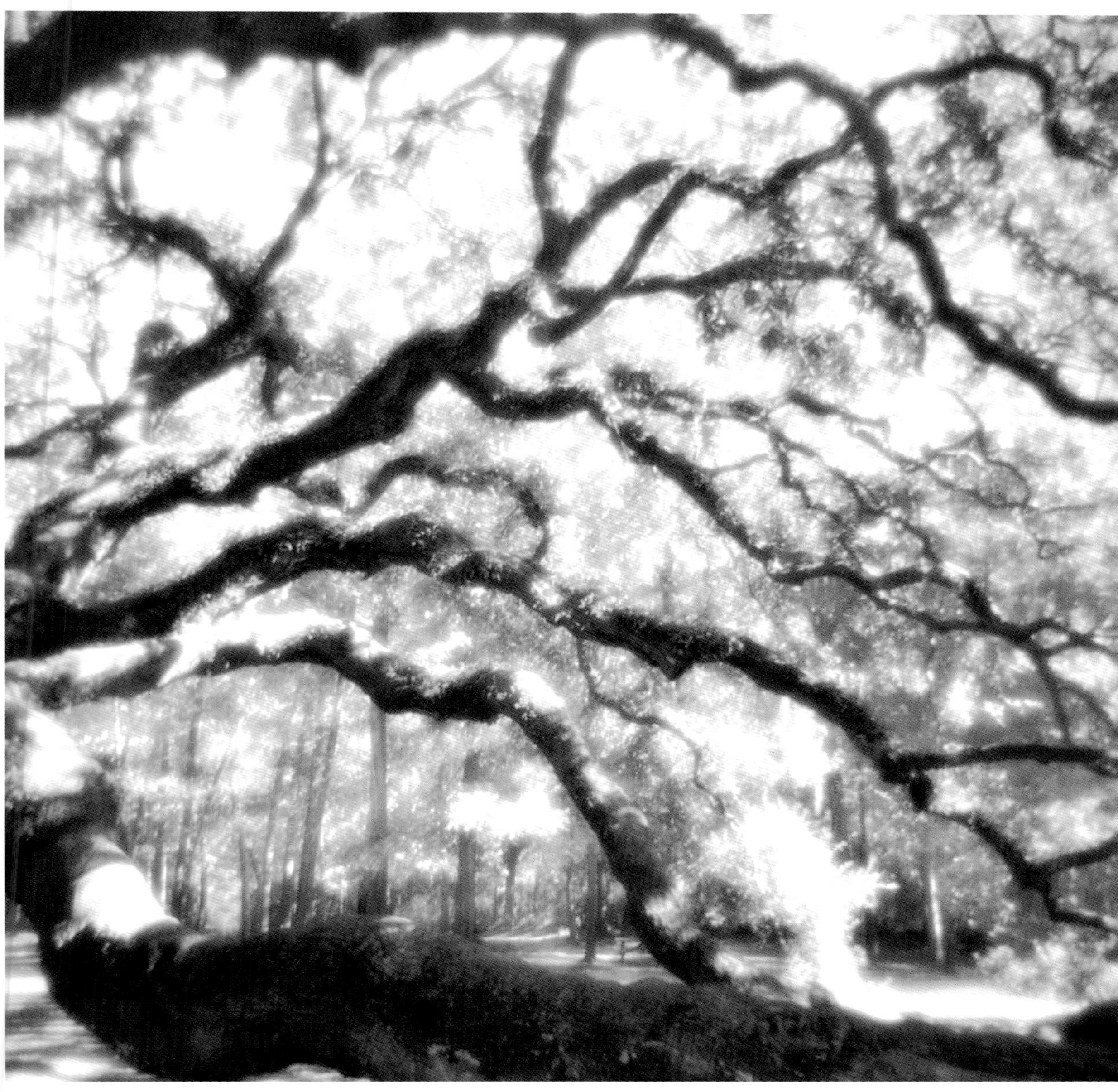

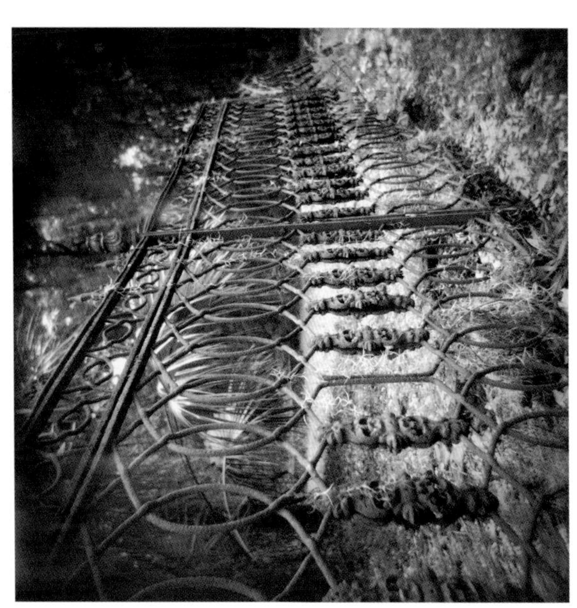

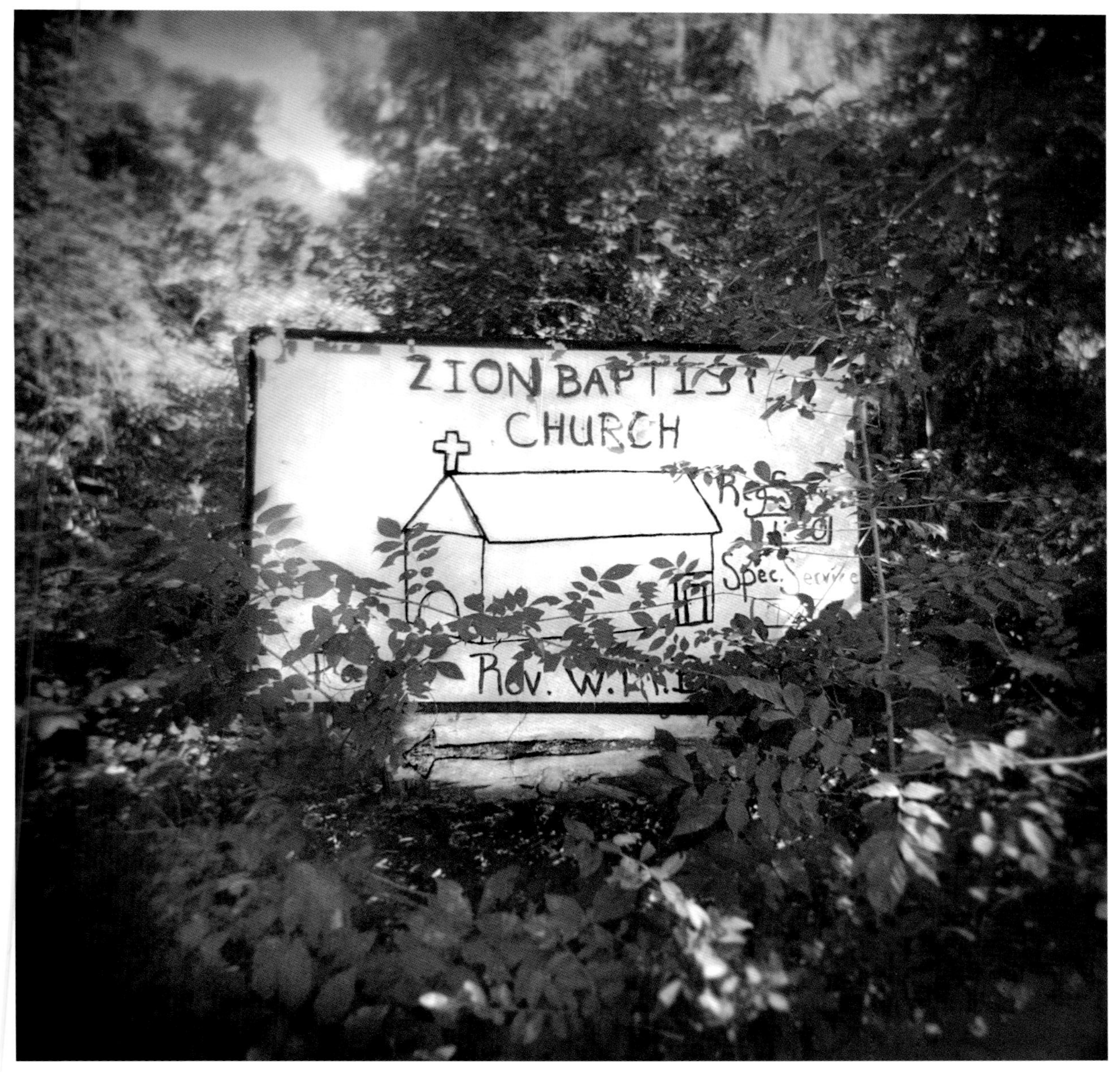
ZION BAPTIST
CHURCH
Spec.

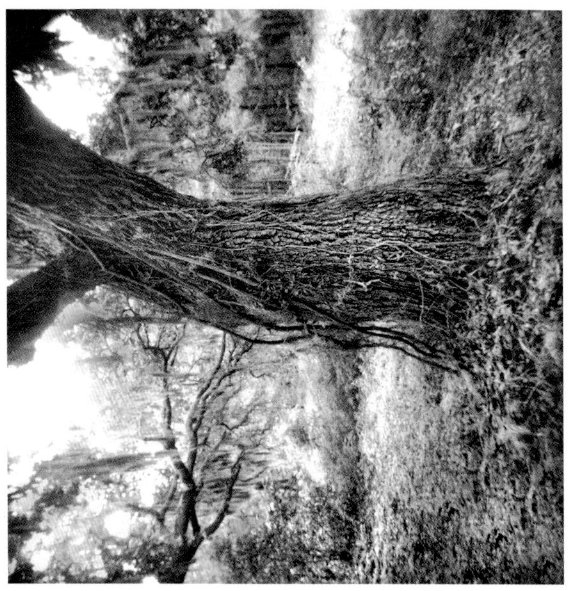
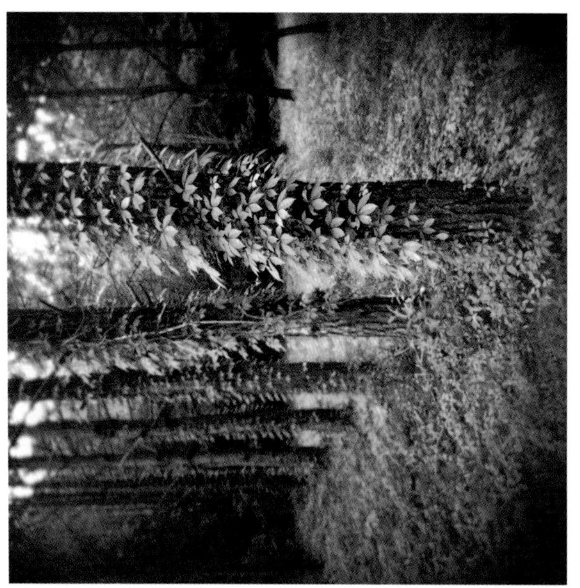
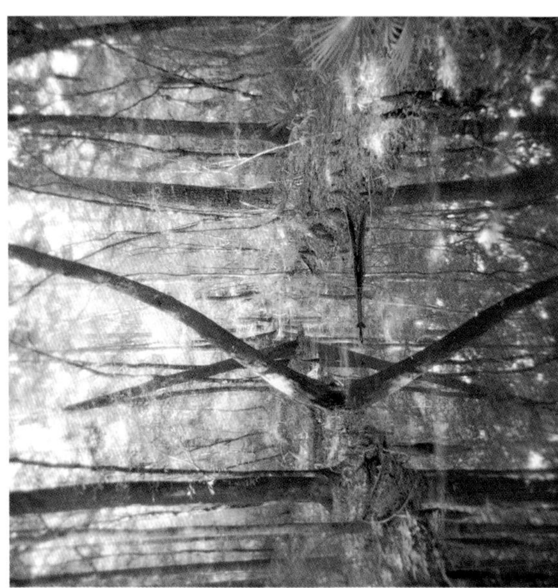
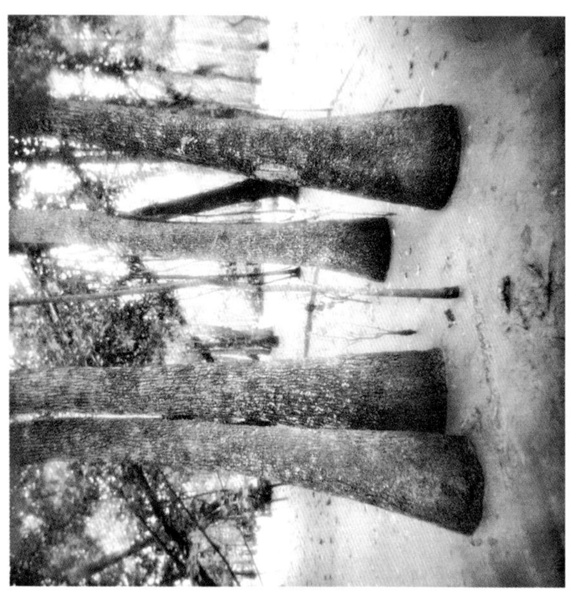

Knees of cypress gurgle up through tannic ooze,
and alligators lurk among the muddy dikes of abandoned rice fields.

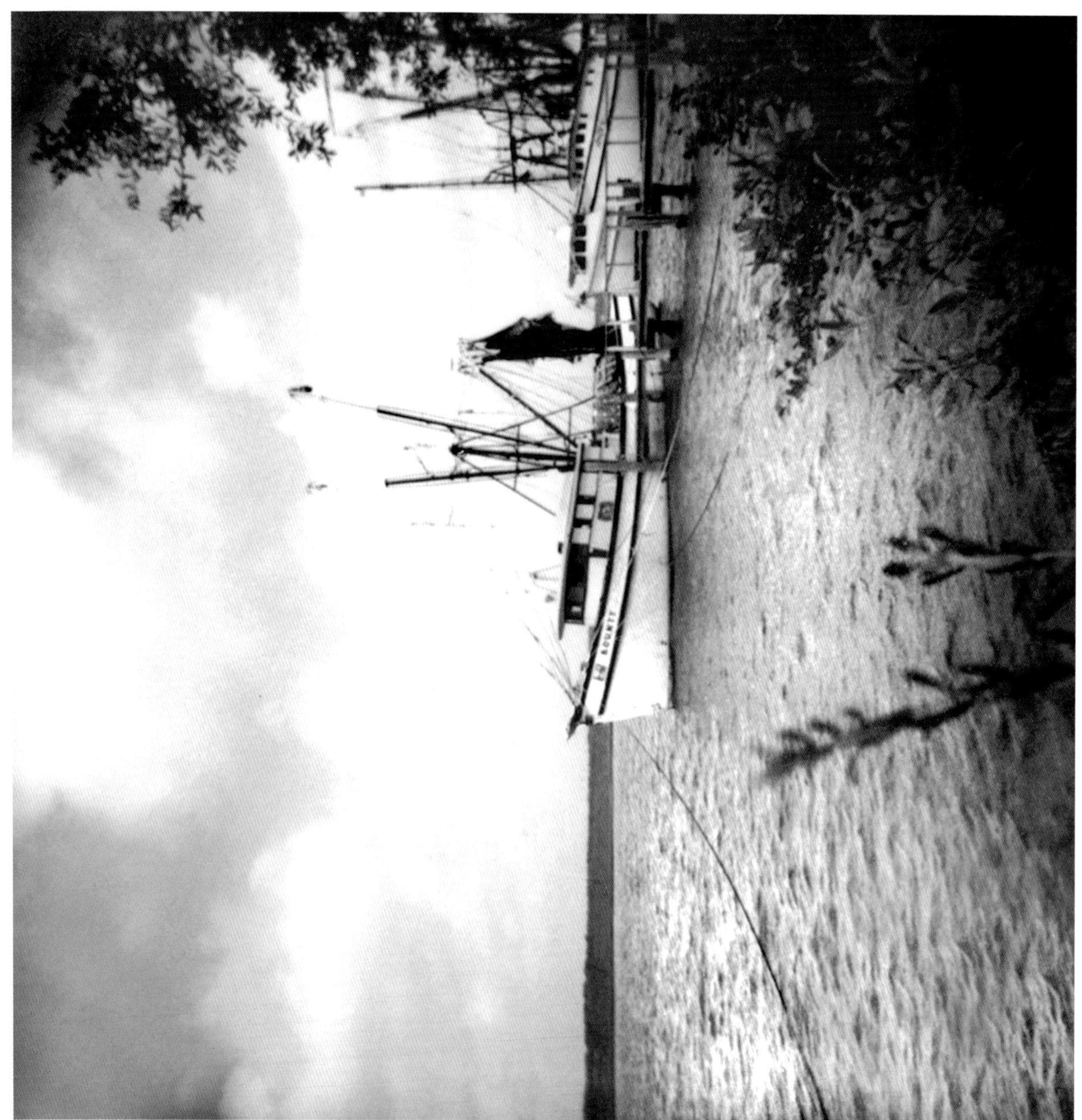

There are no towering mountain peaks, desert sands, high cliffs or deep ravines. The forms here are not as geometric, the views less stratified. It's not so much that the sky is big but more that the water is wide.

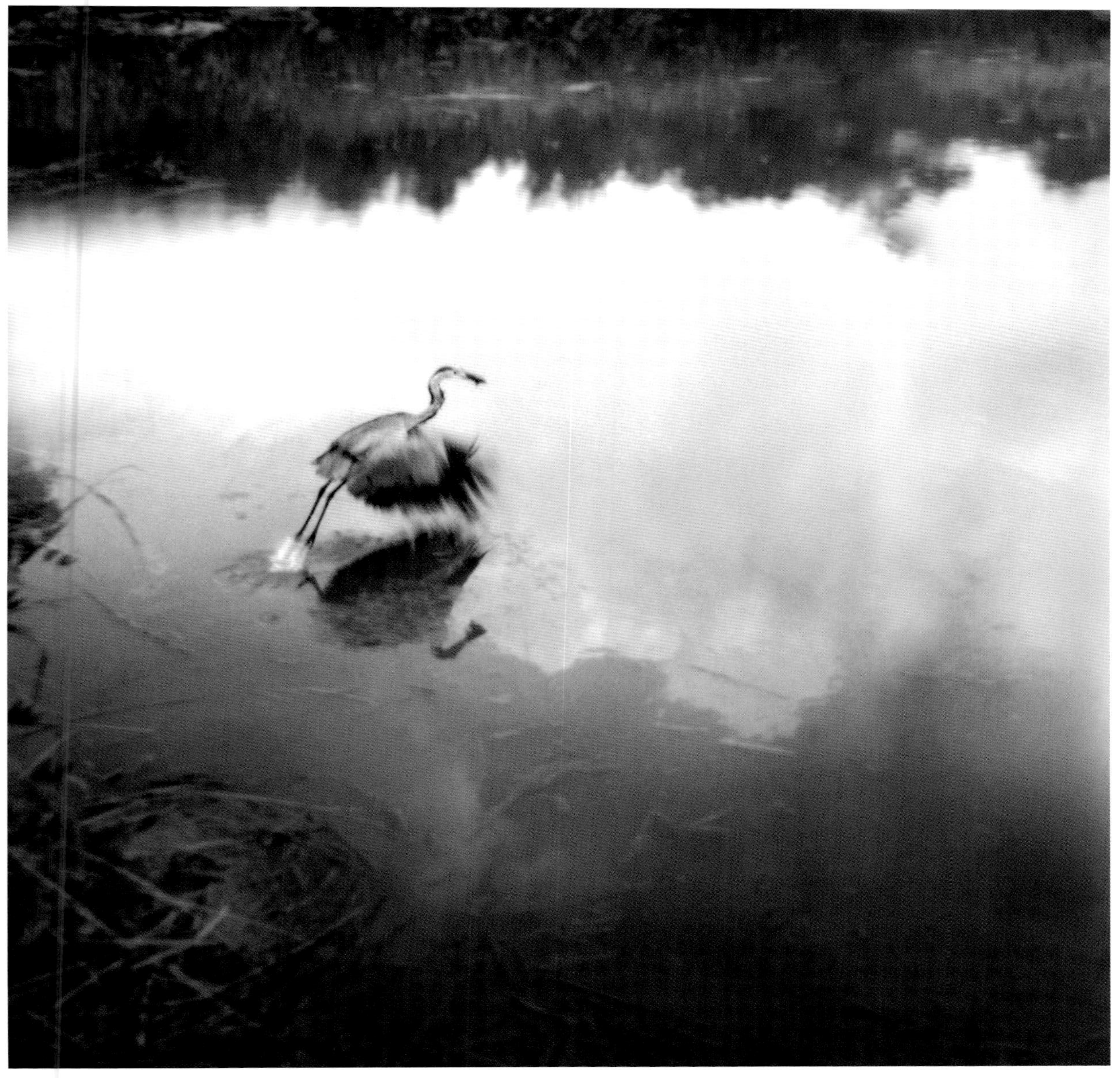

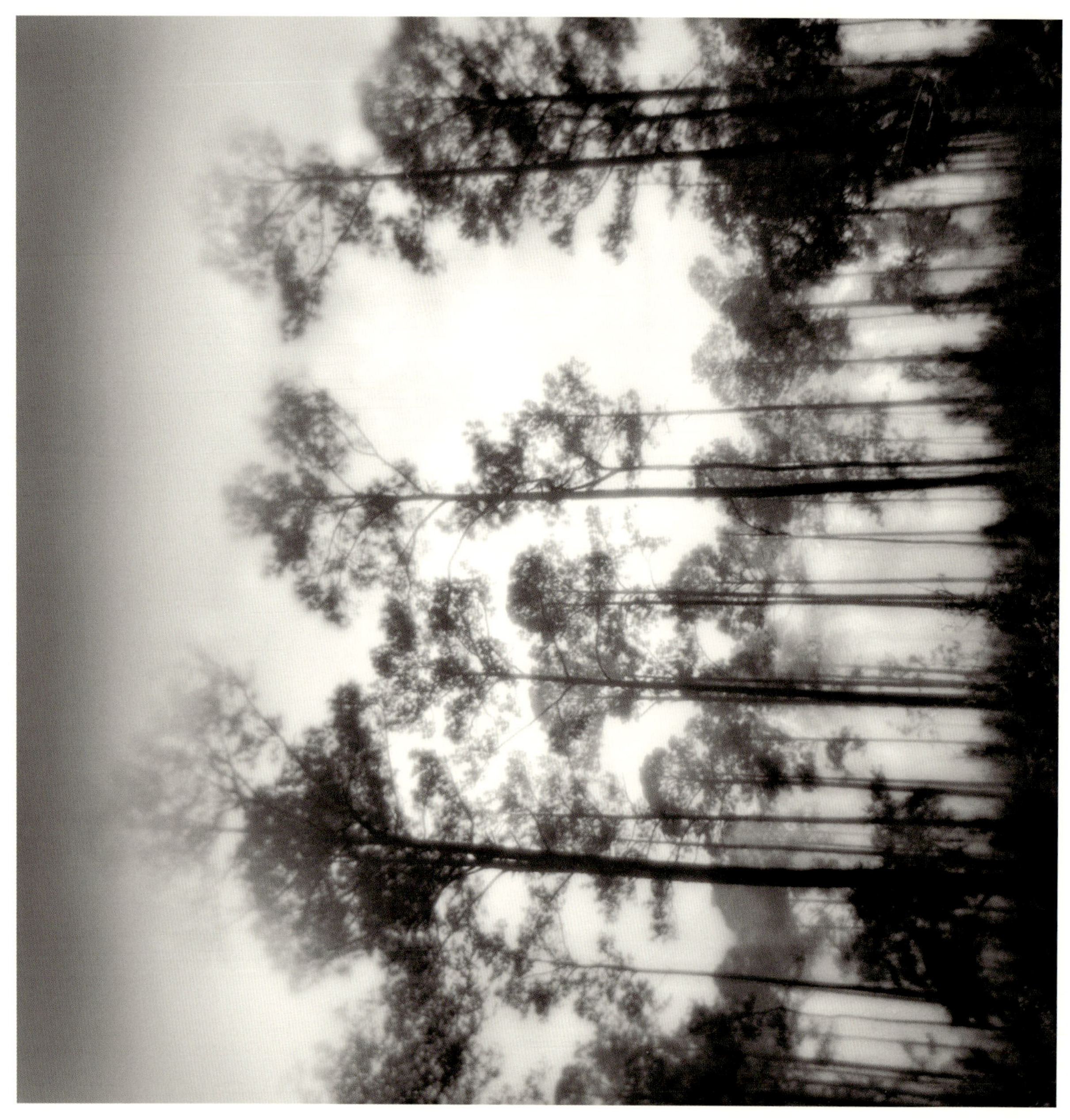

The Lowcountry is subtle and insinuating. Rooted but tenuous. Tarnished and tempting. Impure but forgiving.

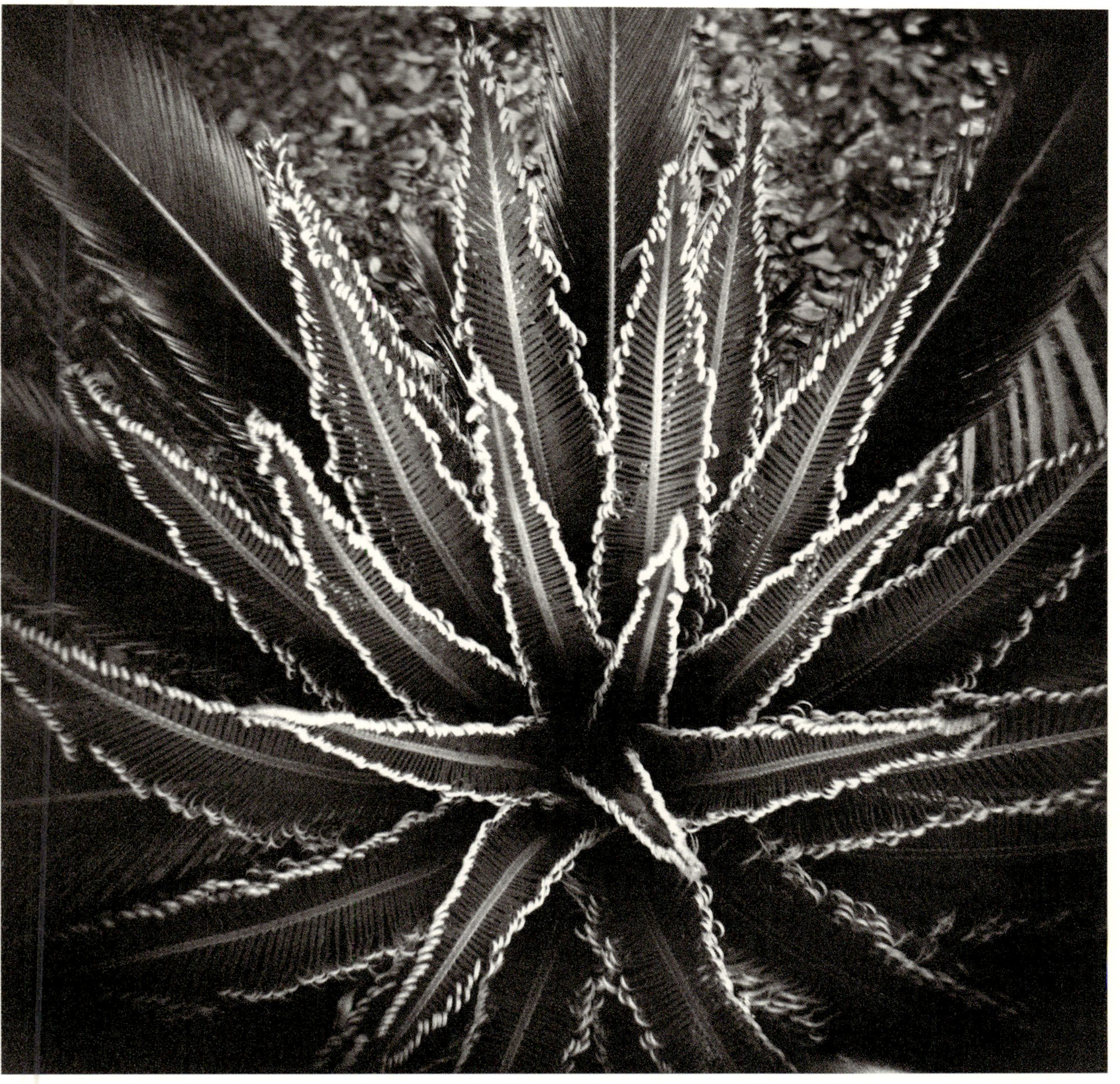

Loosely bound by Savannah to the south and Georgetown to the north, the Lowcountry is riddled with rivers named after its early, native tribes: Combahee, Ashepoo, Edisto and Coosaw. They twist and encircle thousands of islands with names sweeter sung than said: Polawana, Wadamalaw, Warsaw crying out to Half Moon, Distant, Lady's.

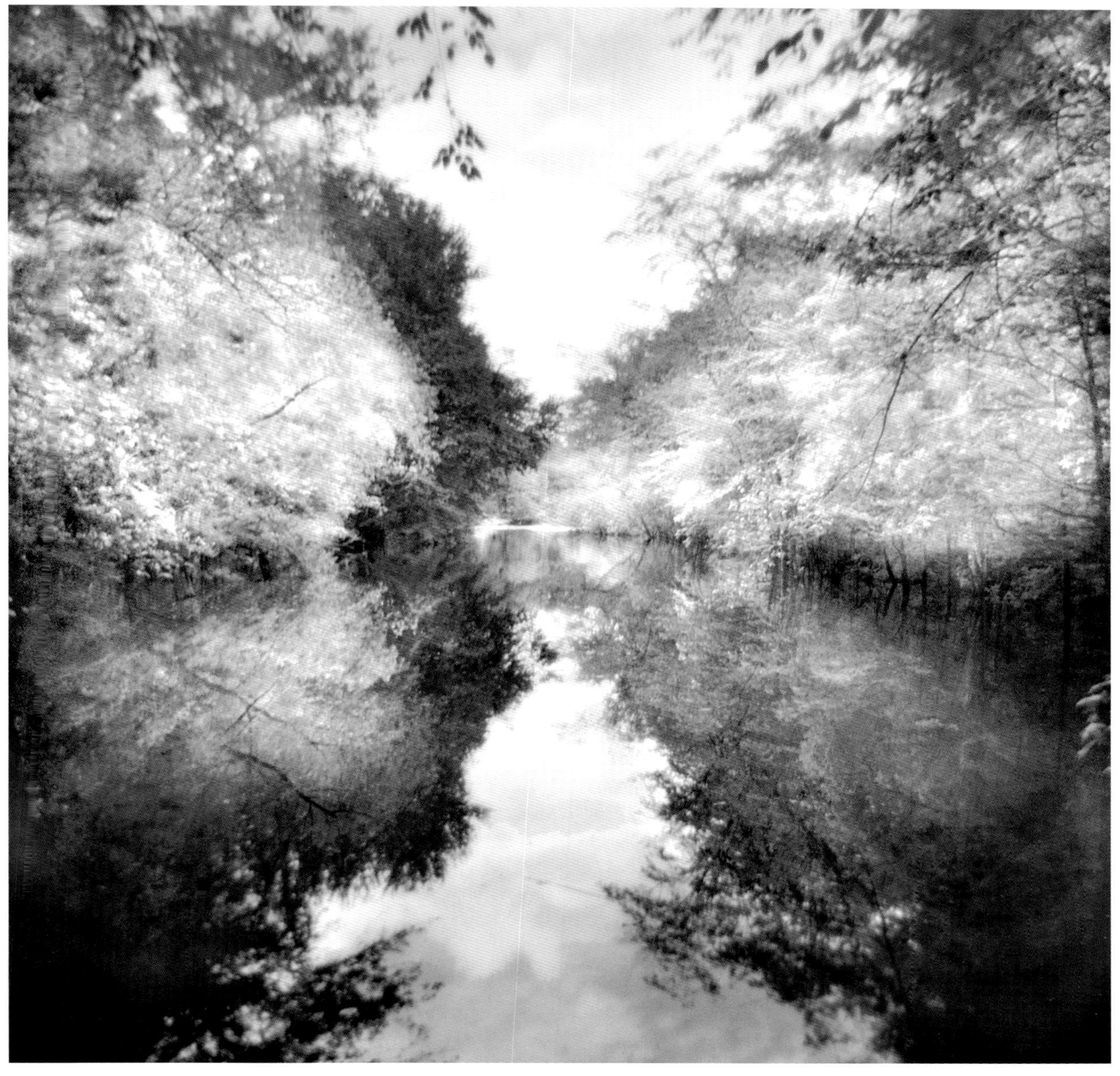

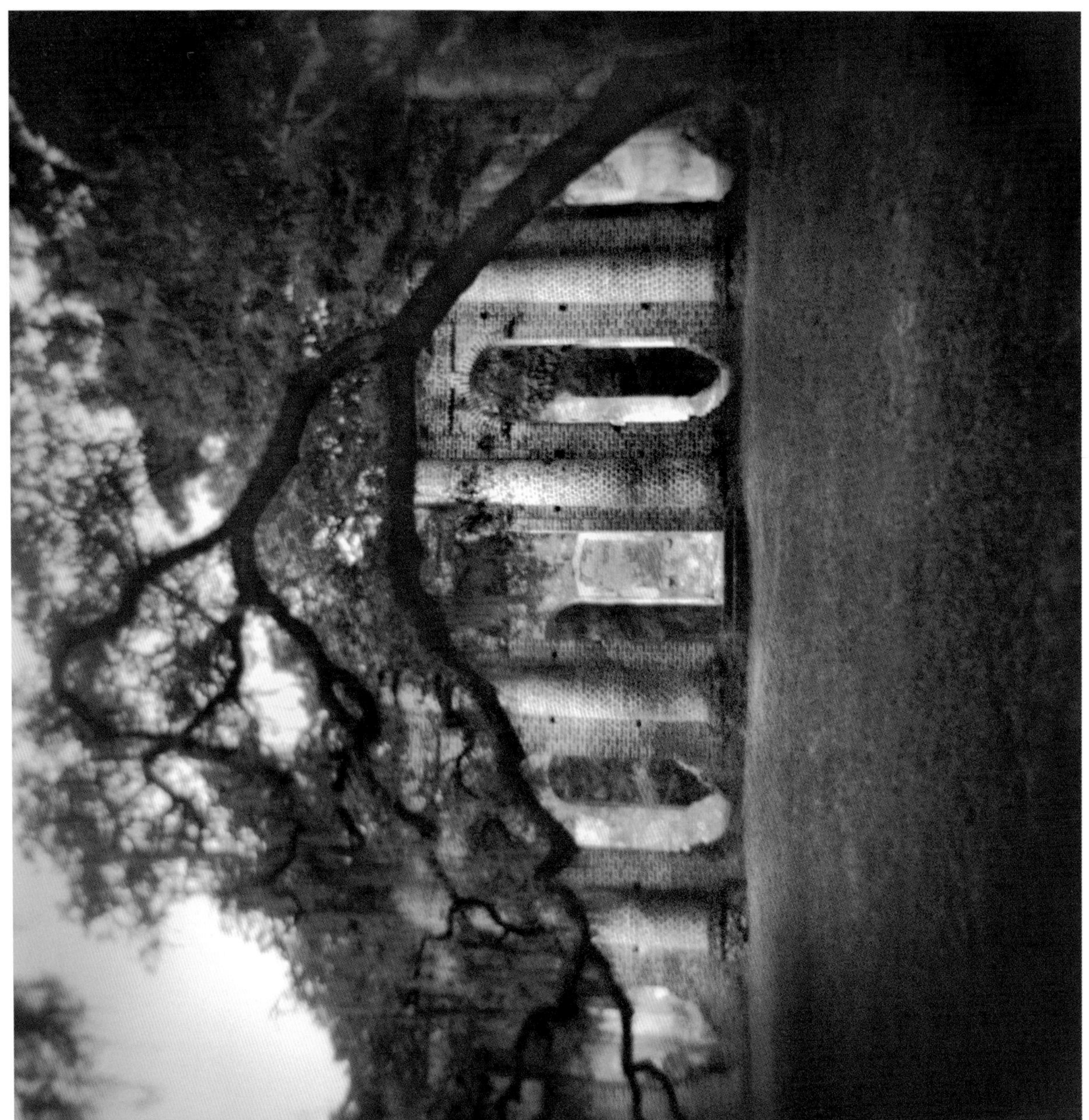

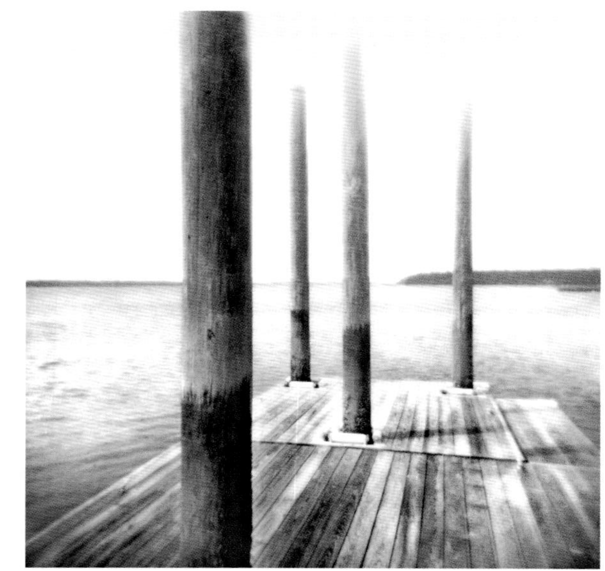

Far from placid tropic dollops in see-through seas, these islands are constantly eroding shorelines and emerging sand bars. They are smothered in mud slicks, scraped with oyster banks and drowned each day by brackish, churning waters darker than a liquid sandstorm. Their geographies are puzzled struggles, tongues of land that jut between rivers called necks and points. Jagged recesses are inlets and cuts.

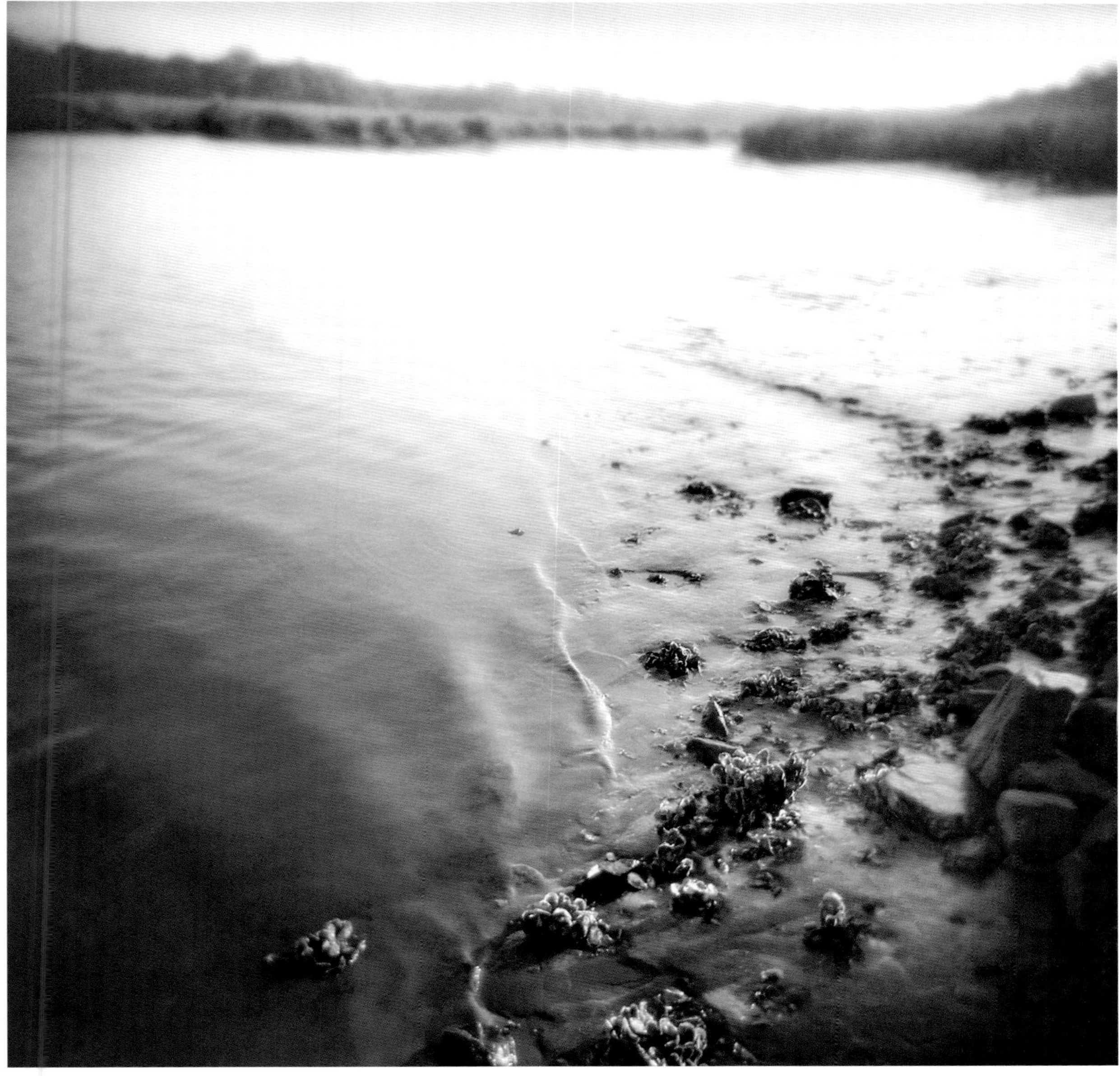

Trees part and rivers bend into watery savannahs of marsh,
emerging and submerging with the patterns of the moon.

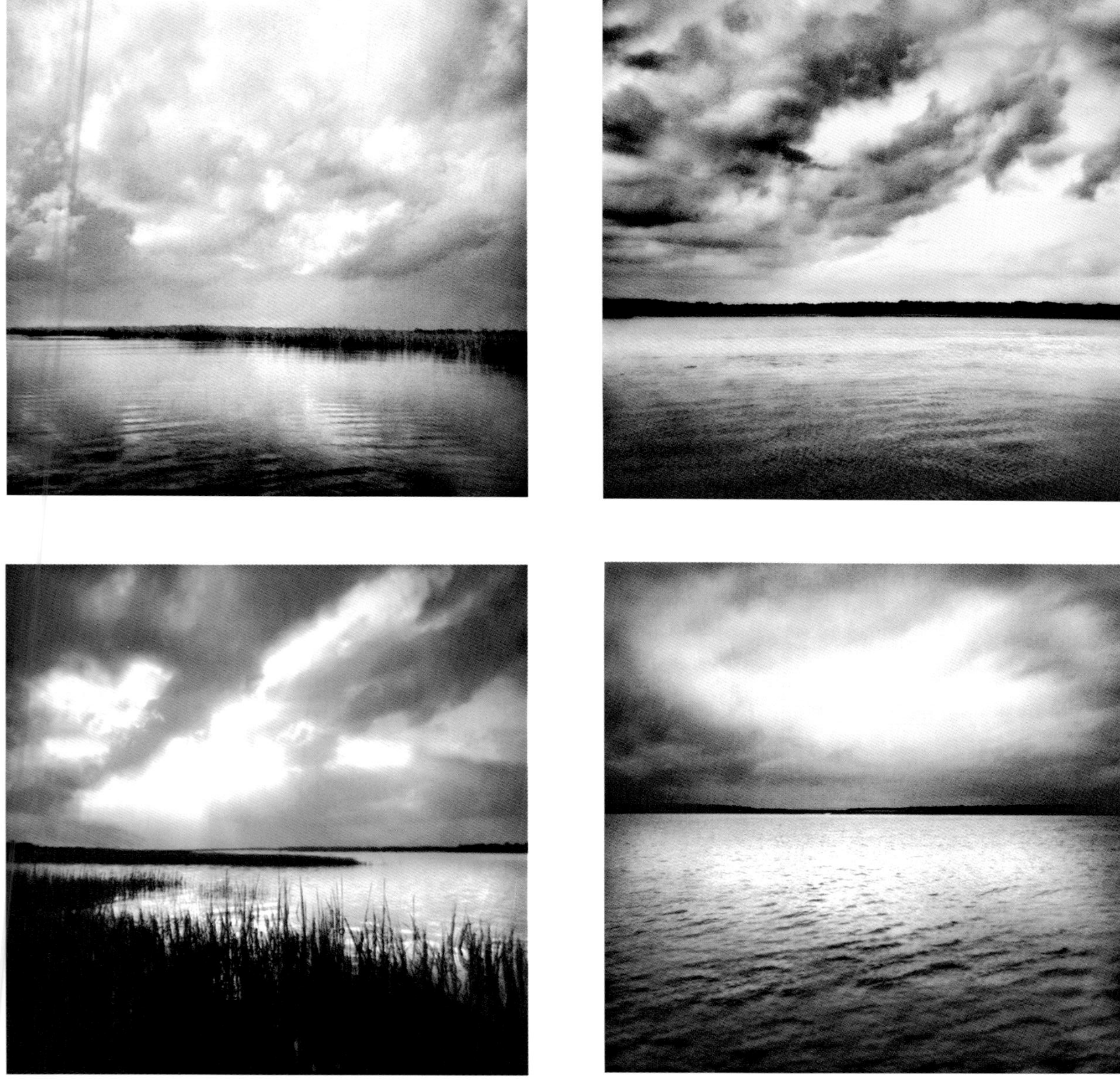

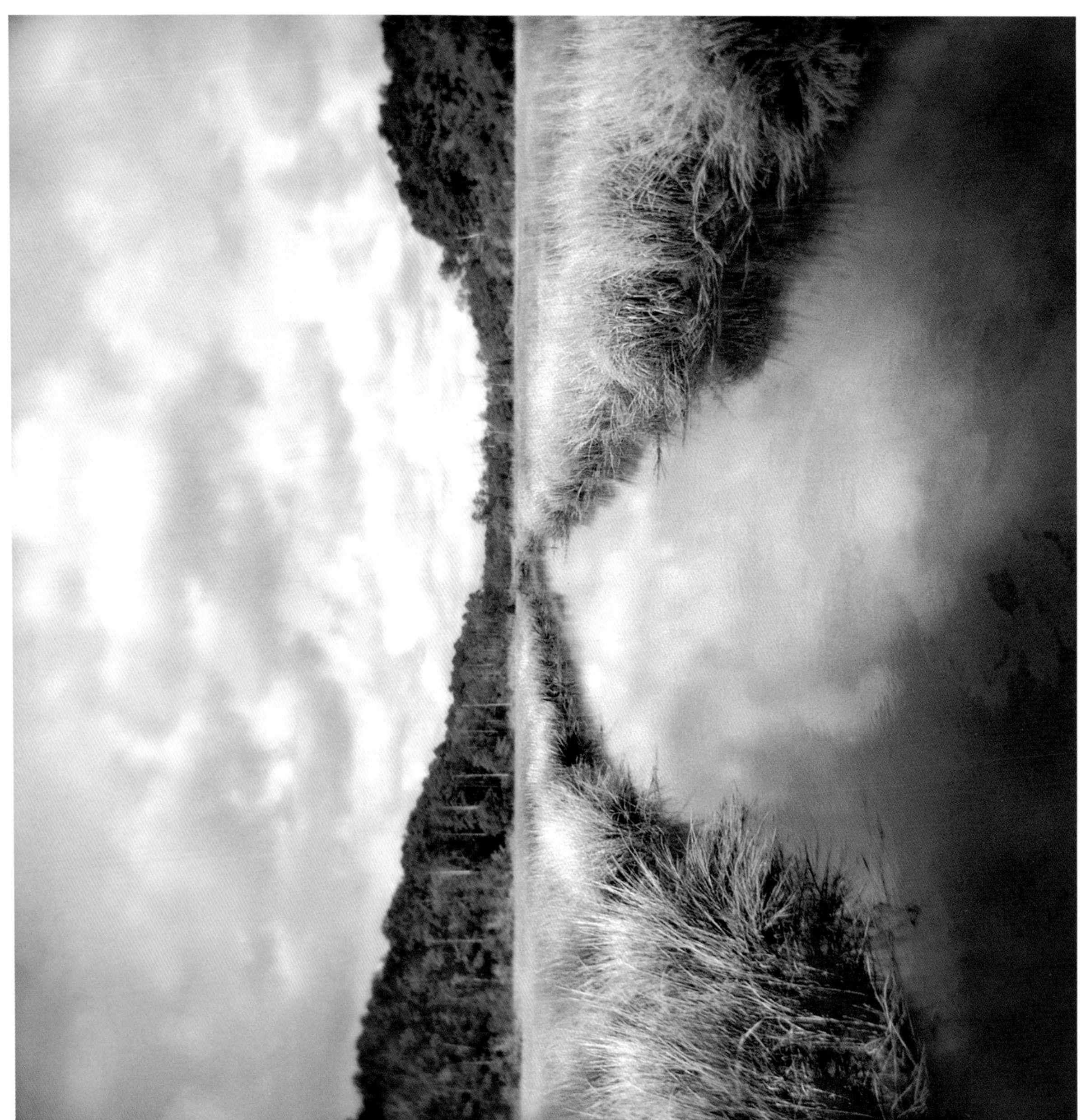

The exact color of the marsh grass depends on the light and the season. On fall mornings finally freed from the swelter of summer, the marsh is a wave of gold set against ribbons of cobalt. In the winter's grey, it warms with the rising sun to dusky pink.

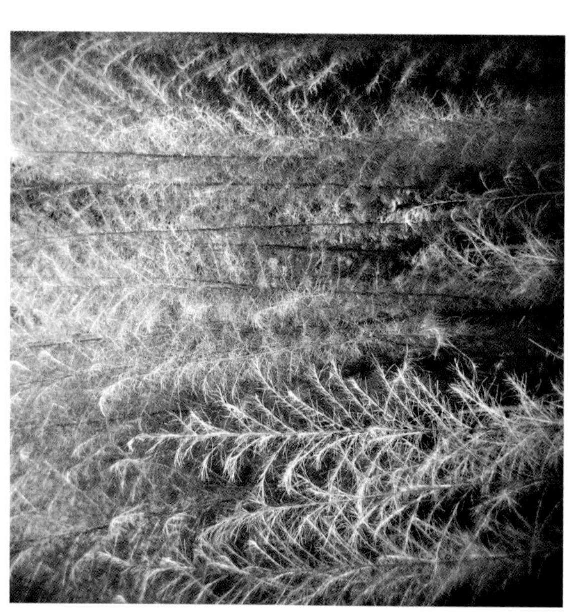

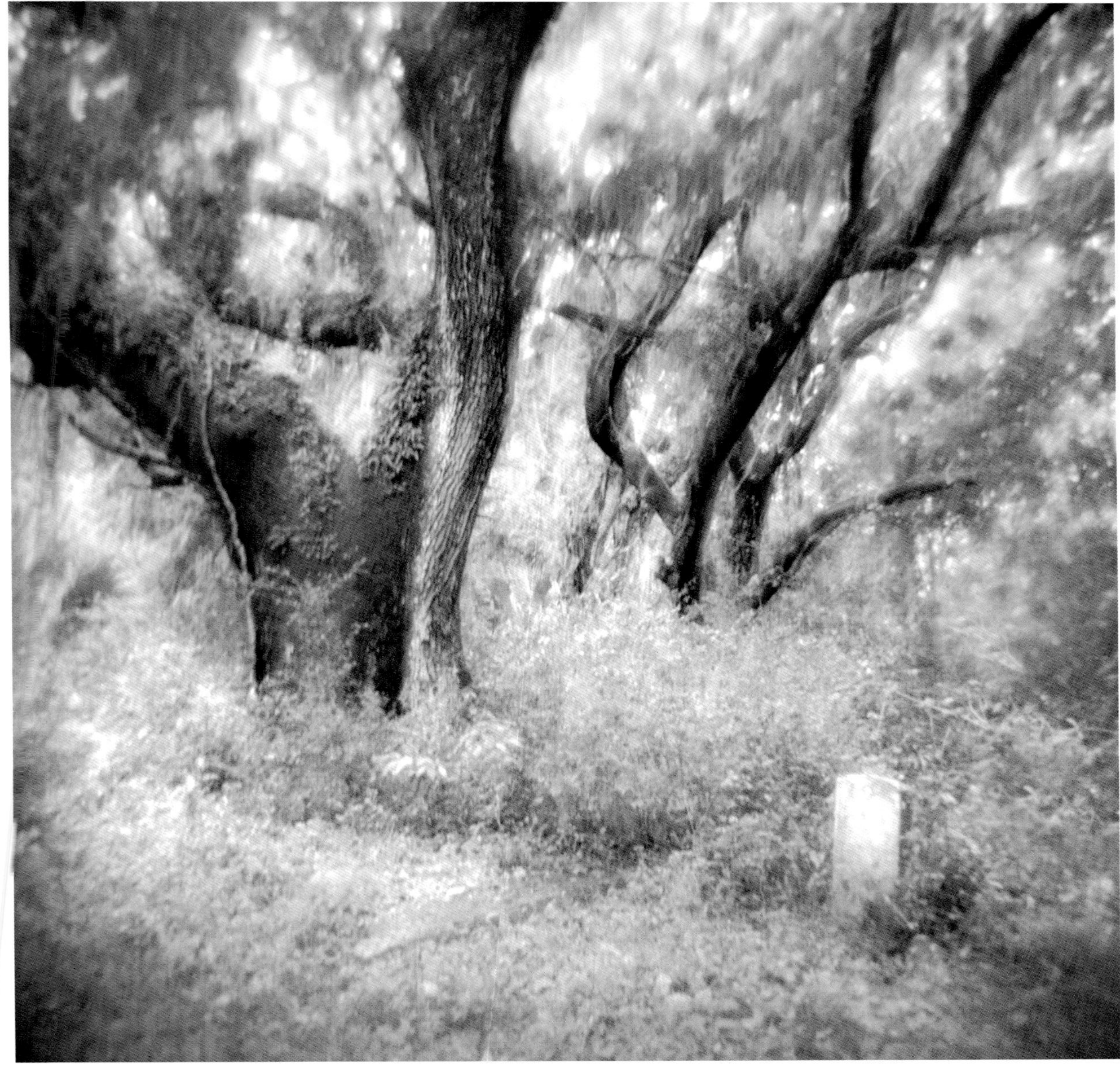

The Gullah people have a saying: "all shut-eye ain't sleep; all goodbye ain't gone." The Lowcountry embodies that ambiguity. It is a place between the sea and high ground, between the past and future. It is neither wild nor truly tame; thoughts here meander between memories and dreams. The presence of the past floats all around. What has gone before is inseparable from what lies ahead, and curious seekers still can find hints and clues to connect the two.

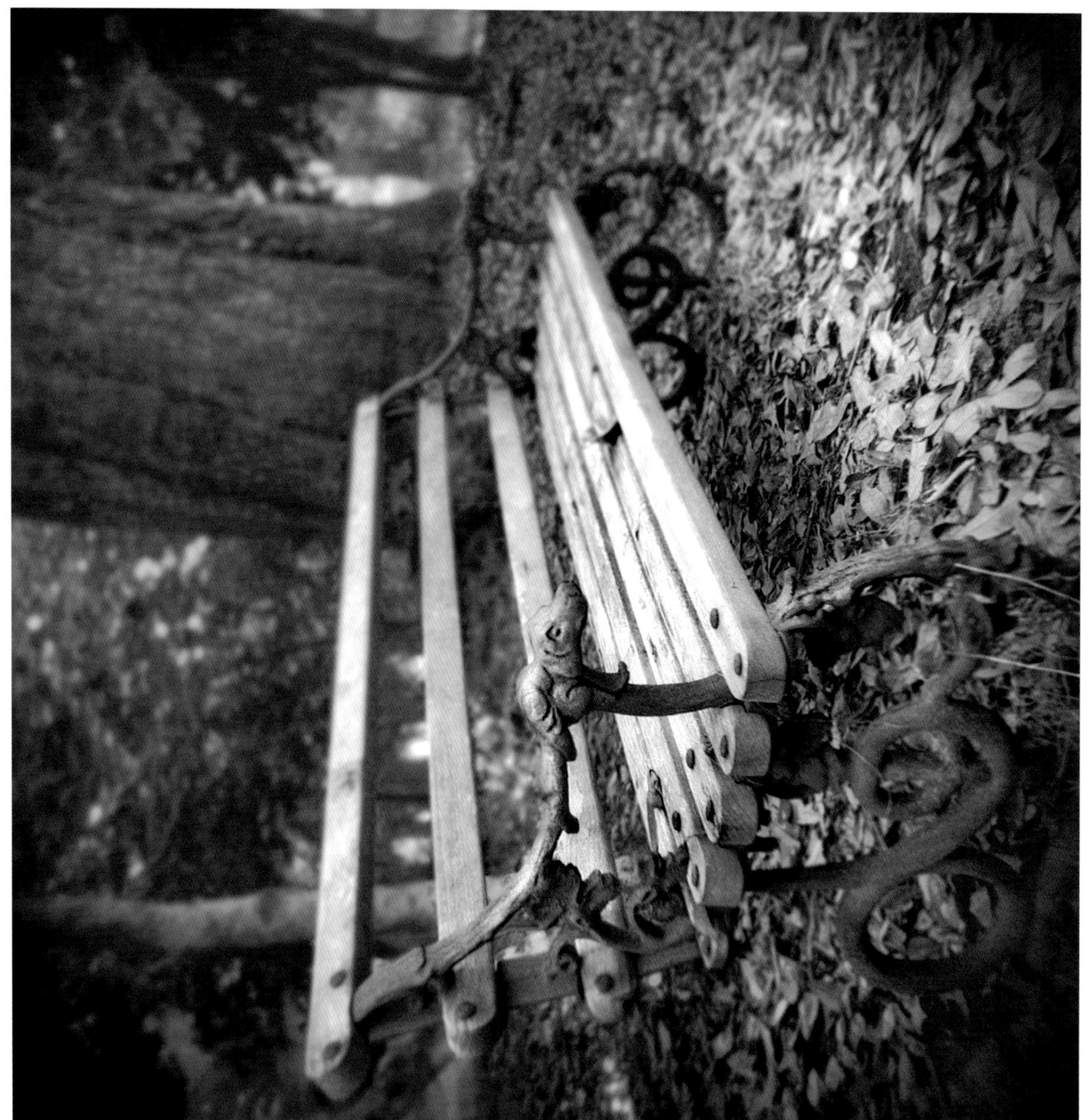

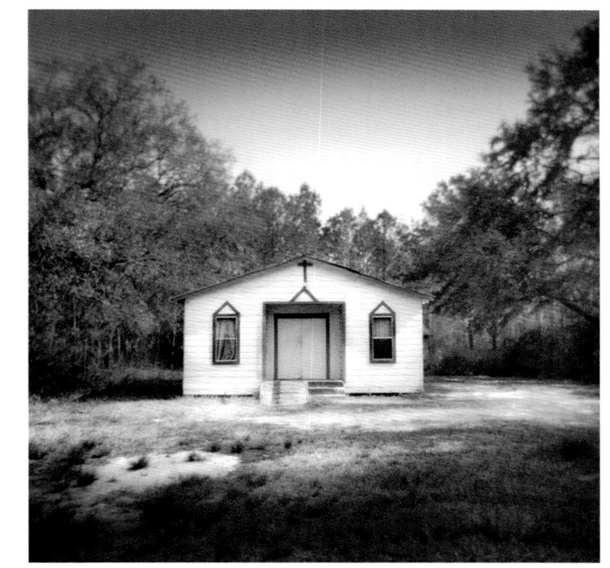

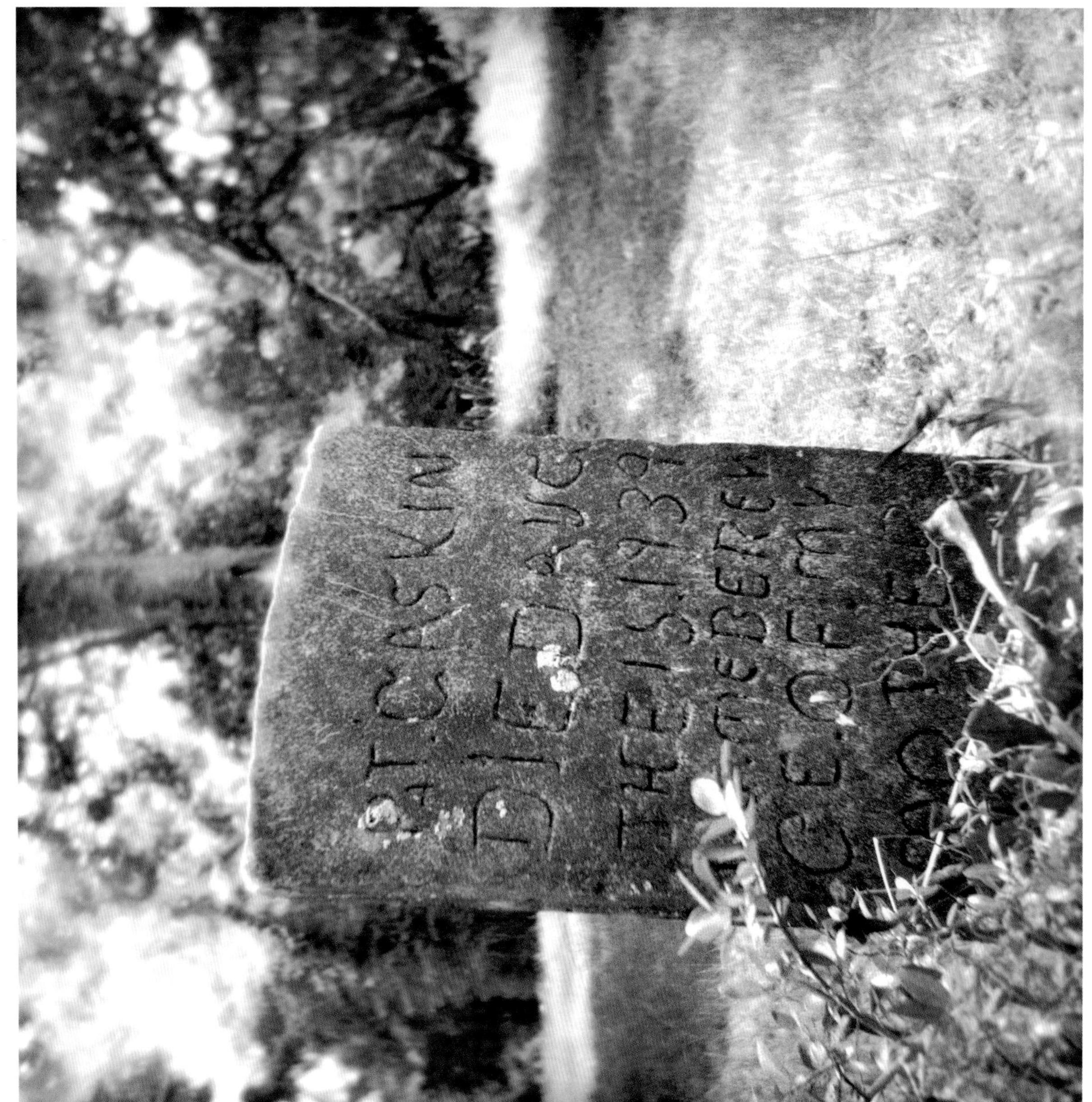

Plantation entrances are arched with parallel lines of live oaks. In older neighborhoods, the faded paint around windows and doors was once "haint" blue, intended to ward off evil spirits. Development stops at water's edge, and new homes are held off by hand-carved headstones – as if African ancestors demanded a path home, each spirit claiming a sacred launching place, however small.

Connections to the past are easily overlooked: the claw of a crypt in an overgrown cemetery, the stump of a dock piling in the marsh. But if spirits linger anywhere, it surely must be in the Lowcountry. The creak of an iron gate swinging in the wind could be a presence passing through. Rusty folding chairs outside a liquor store are worn from generations of bottles passed and tales told. Swamp gas in the marshes at land's end are said to light the night sky with glowing spheres of mystery.

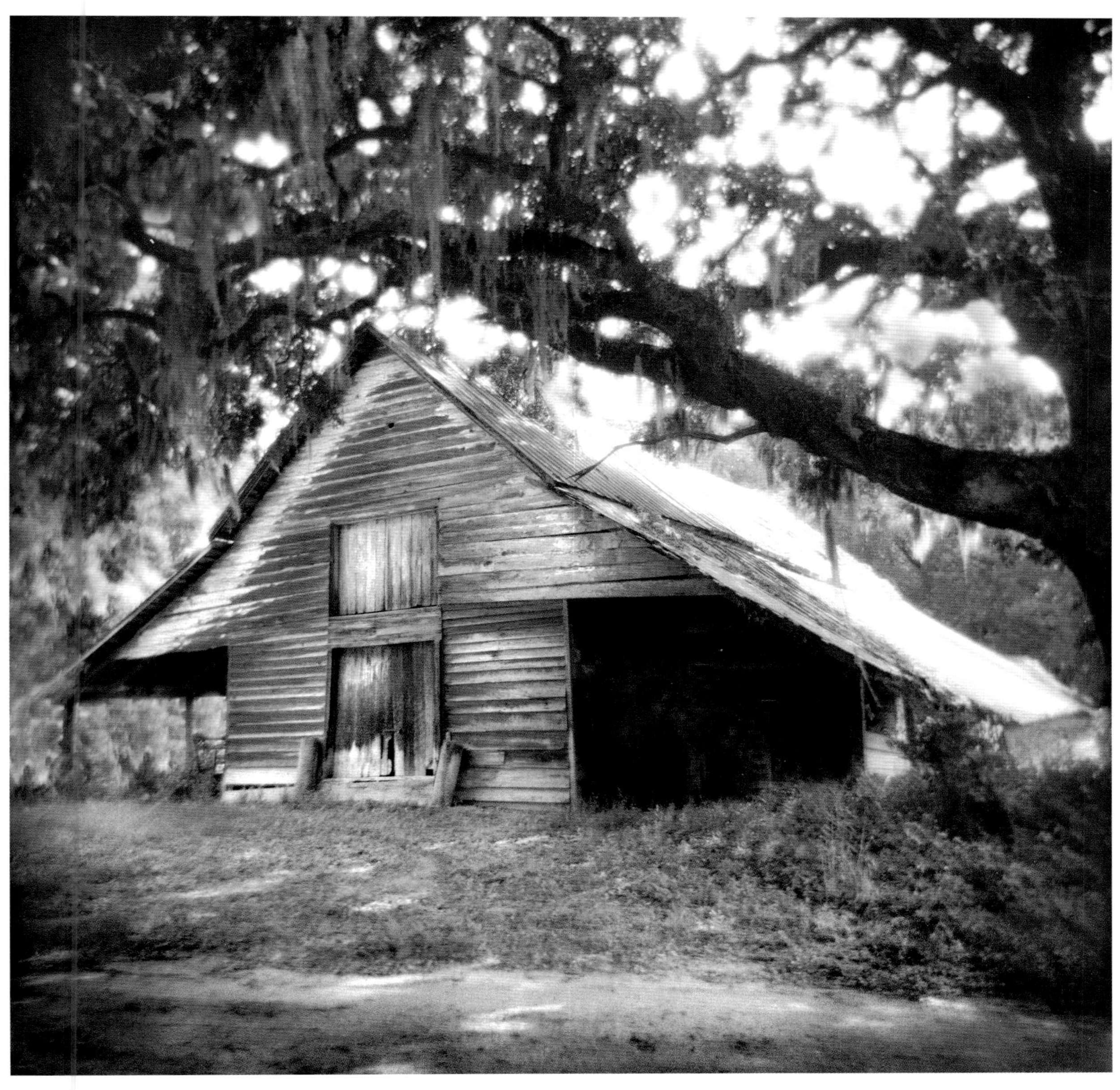

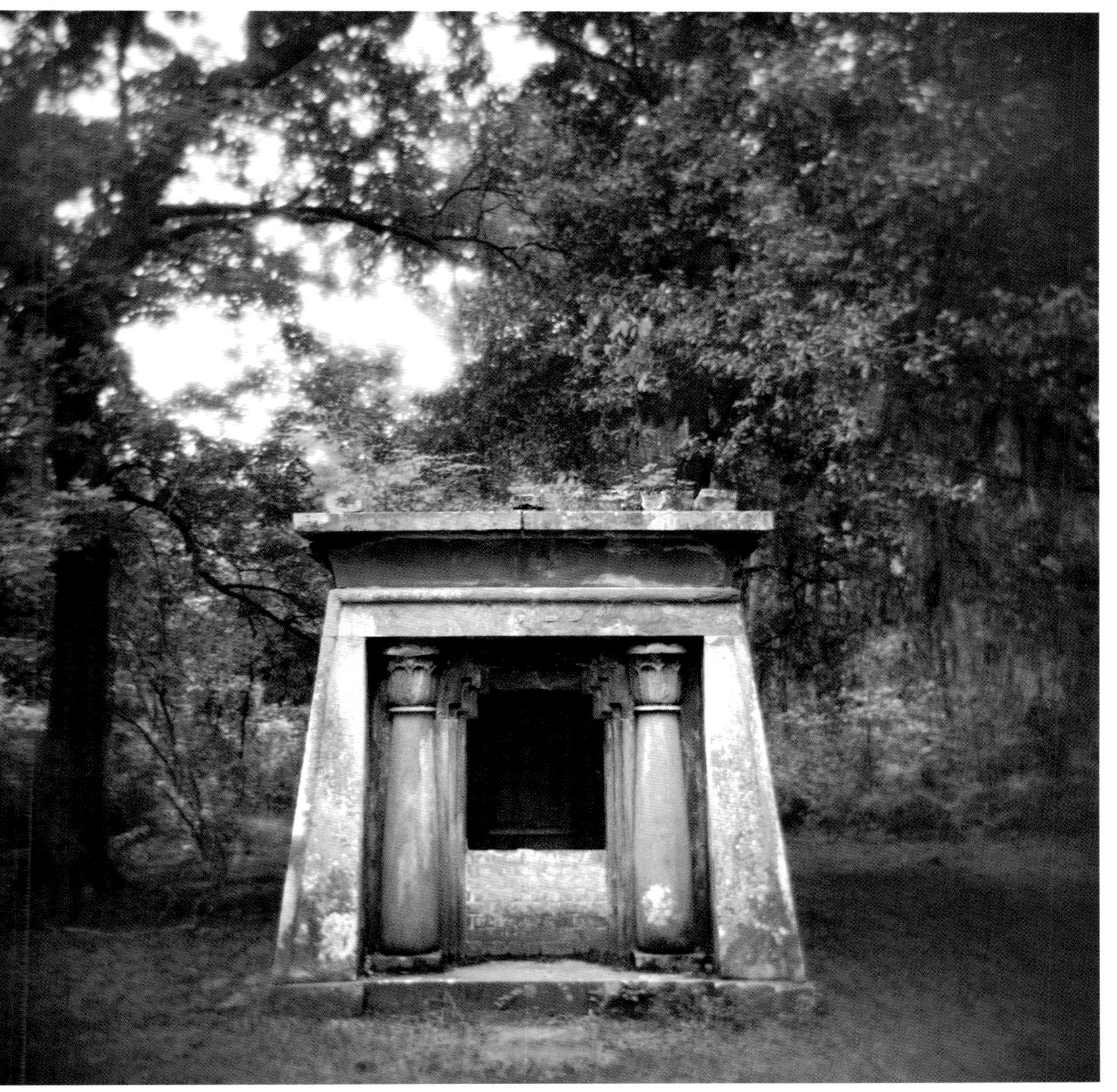

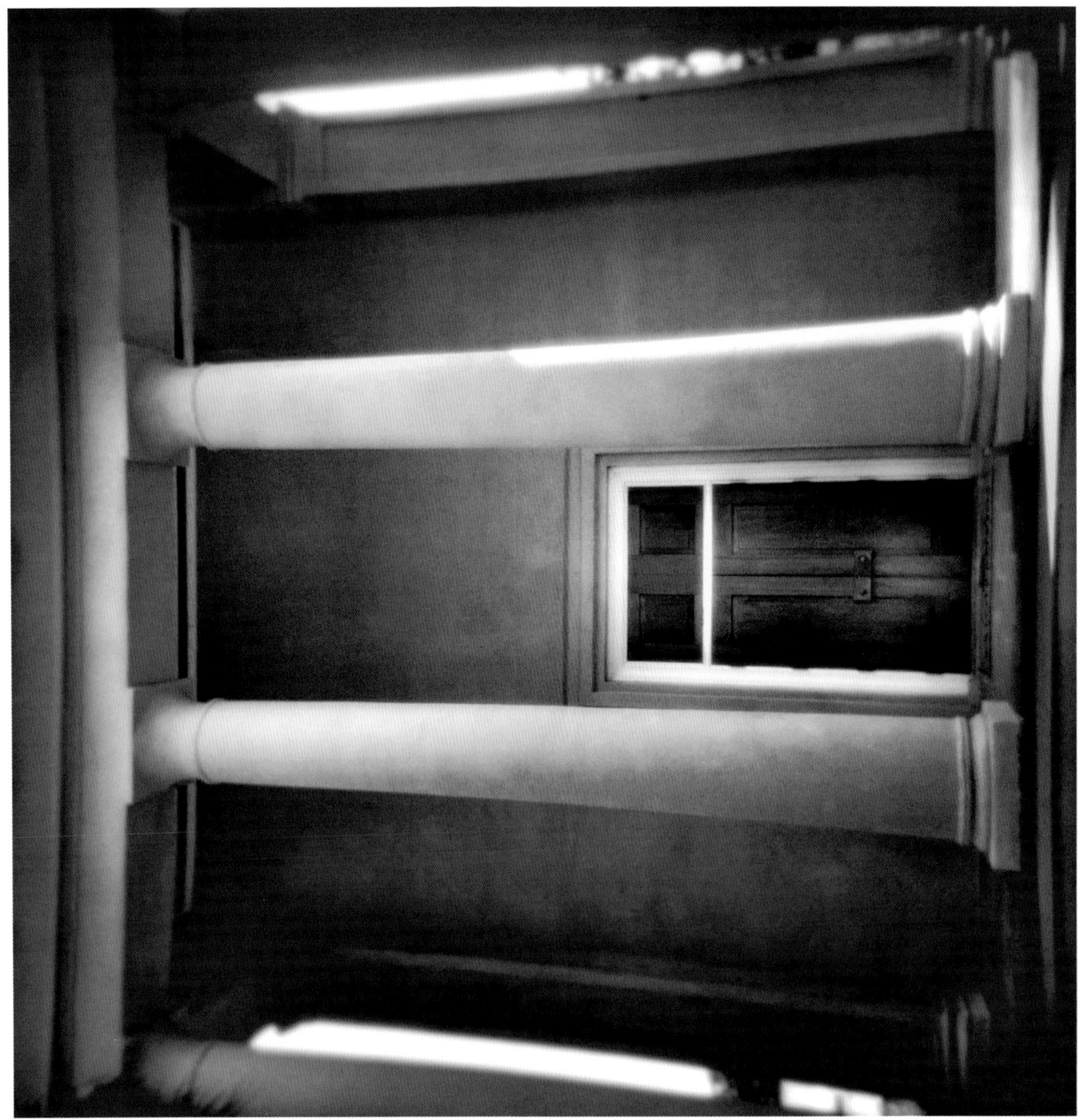

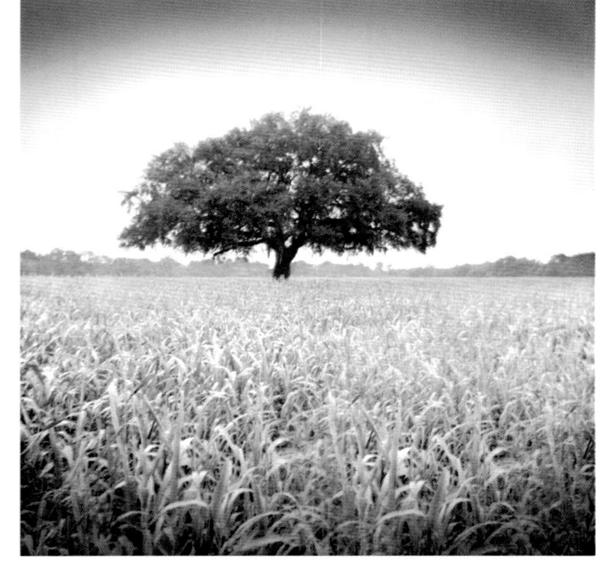

The sound track of the past still drifts through the heavy air: the clank of shrimp nets on piers in September, the snip of pruning shears after the spring azaleas bloom. It is hummed in wretches saved and heard in hearts blessed.

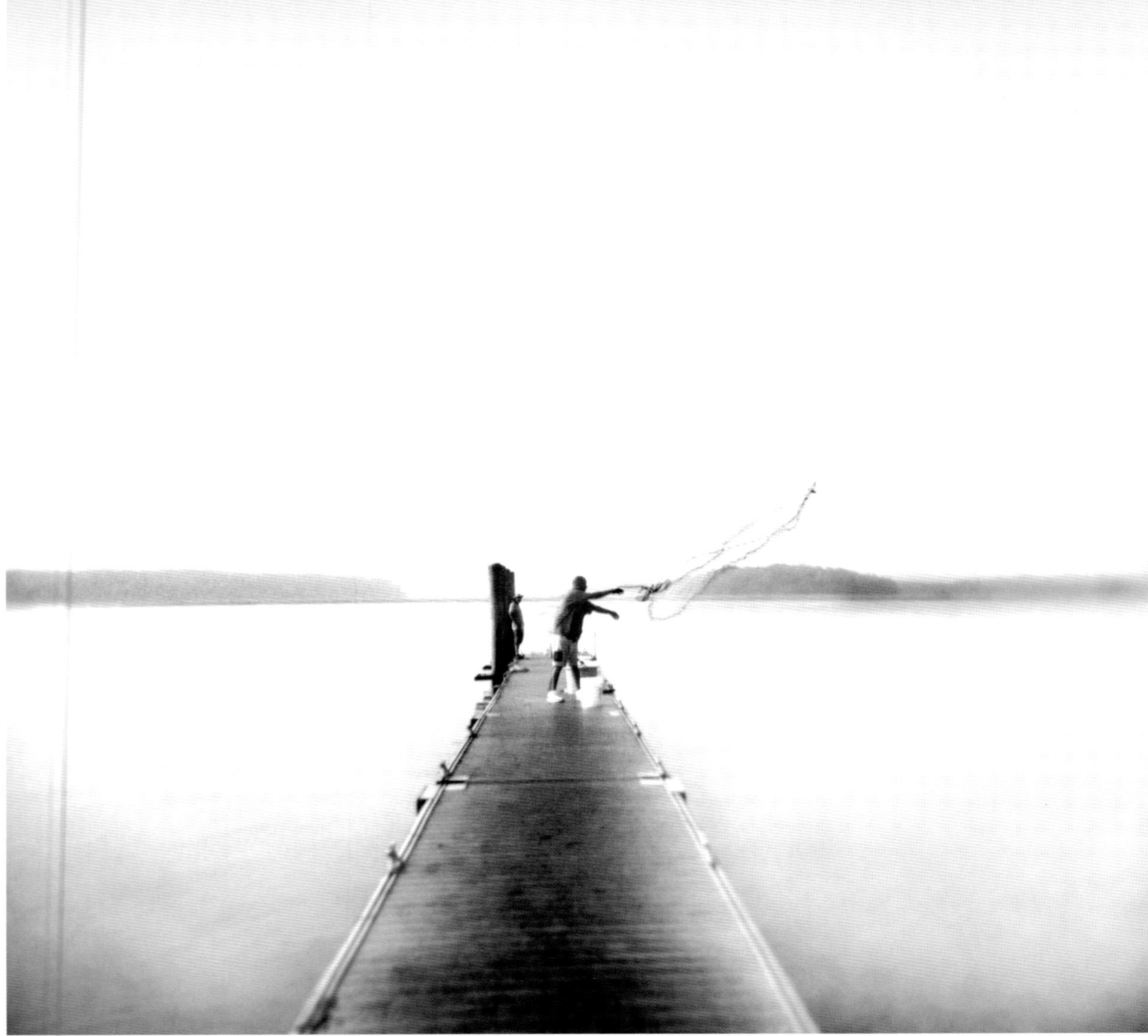

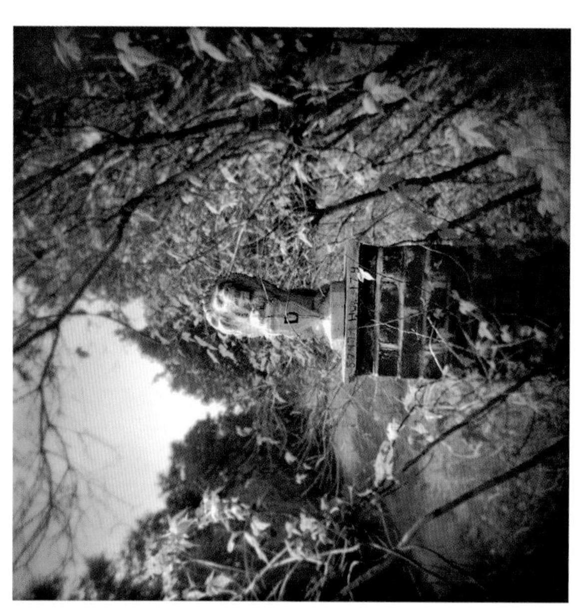

These whispers from the past become harder for us to hear; that is clear. Why this is so is less transparent. Among the Gullah people, only now are traditions celebrated. Before they became "heritage," they were just things done the way they'd always been. Praise houses weren't considered praiseworthy, nor the culture, cultured. The language spoken at home did not belong in public. Heirs couldn't pool enough resources to pay the rising taxes on undeveloped island property. Opportunity and anonymity pulled even rooted youth north like magnets to an opposite pole. There they prospered, married and created a history not so entangled and divided by the waters.

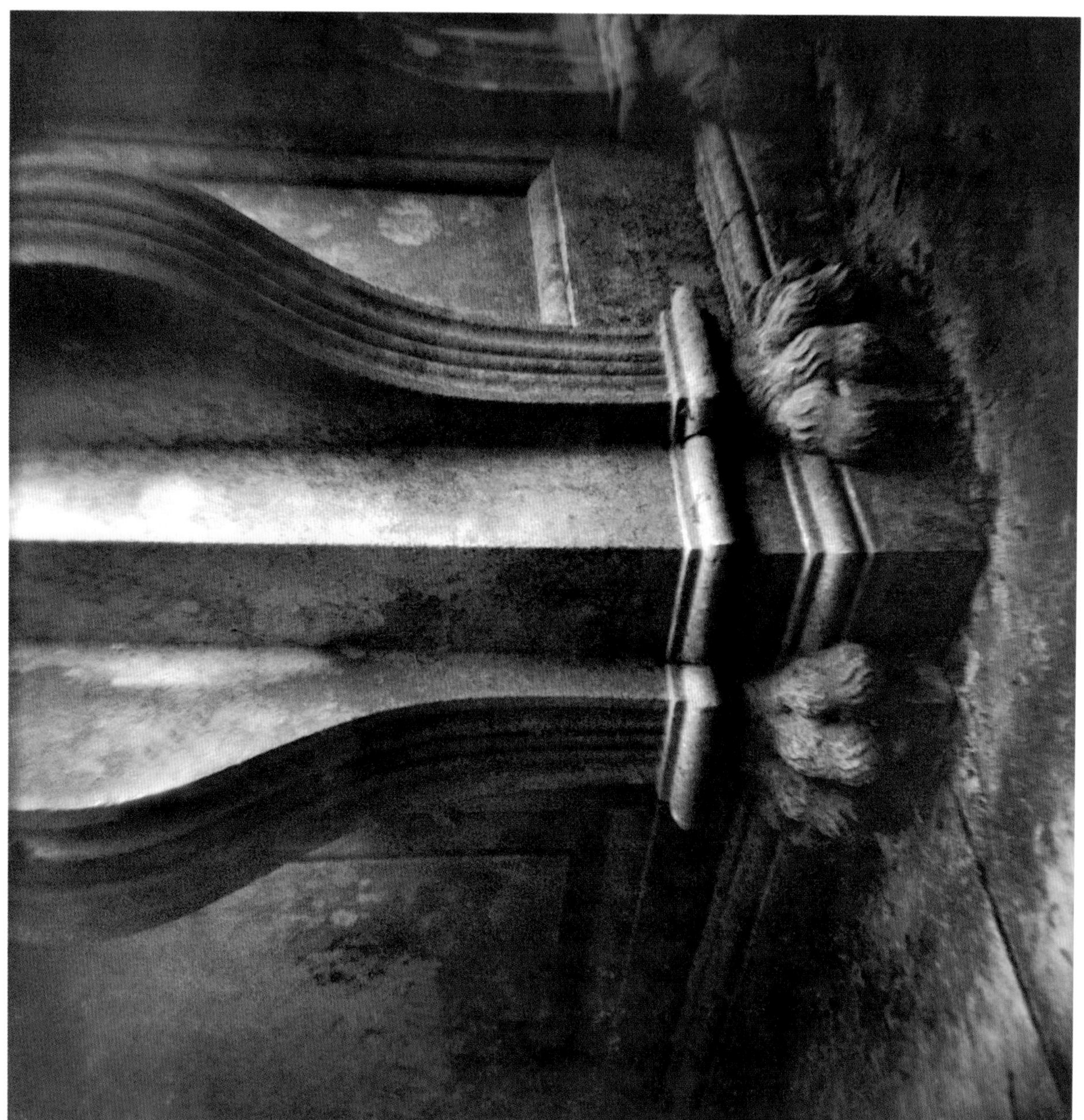

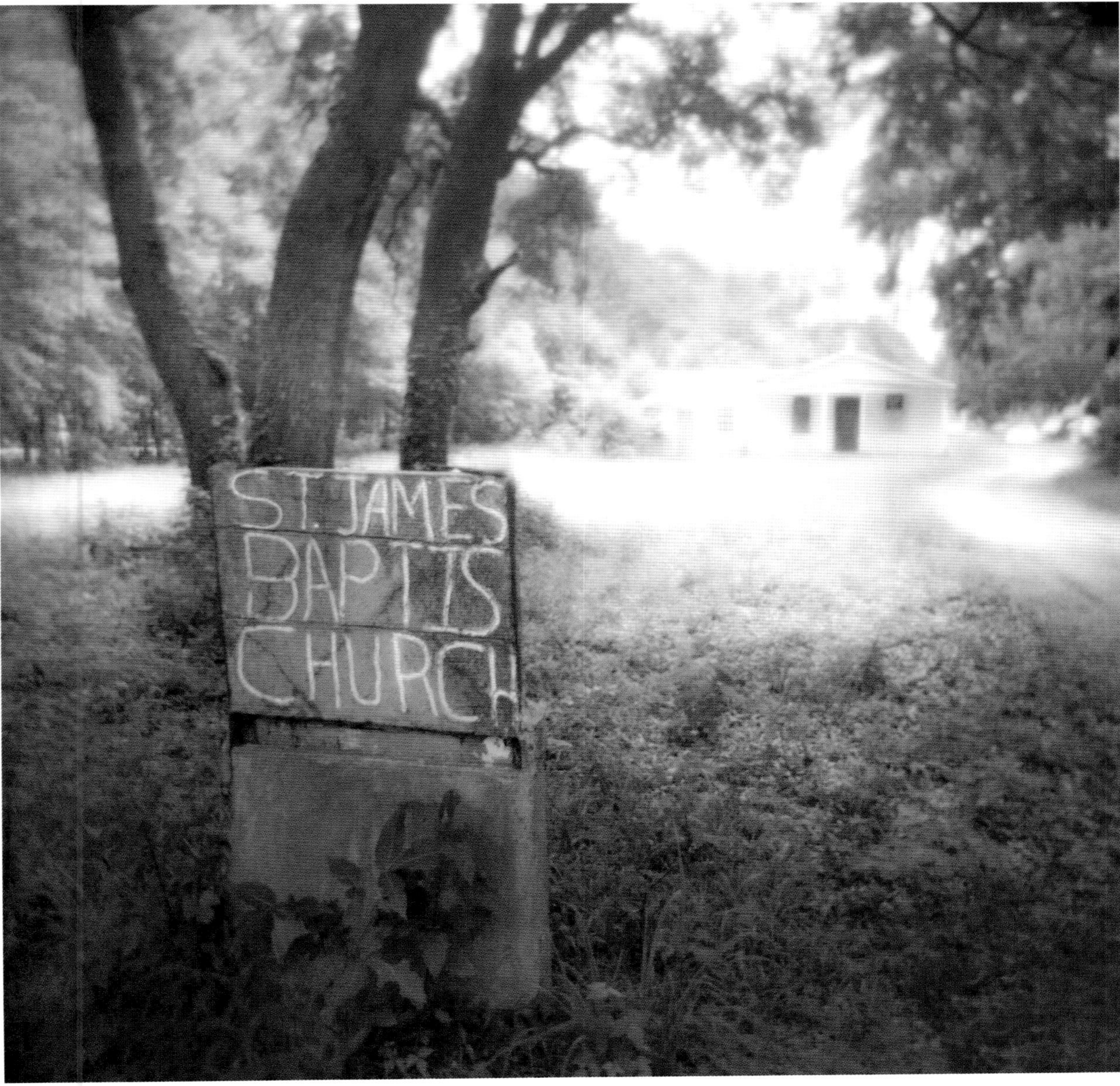
ST. JAMES
BAPTIS
CHURCH

Islands once mostly black are quickly fading. Seasons pass, and the only constant is change. What was distant becomes developed. What was remote is now private. What once was ignored is suddenly coveted.

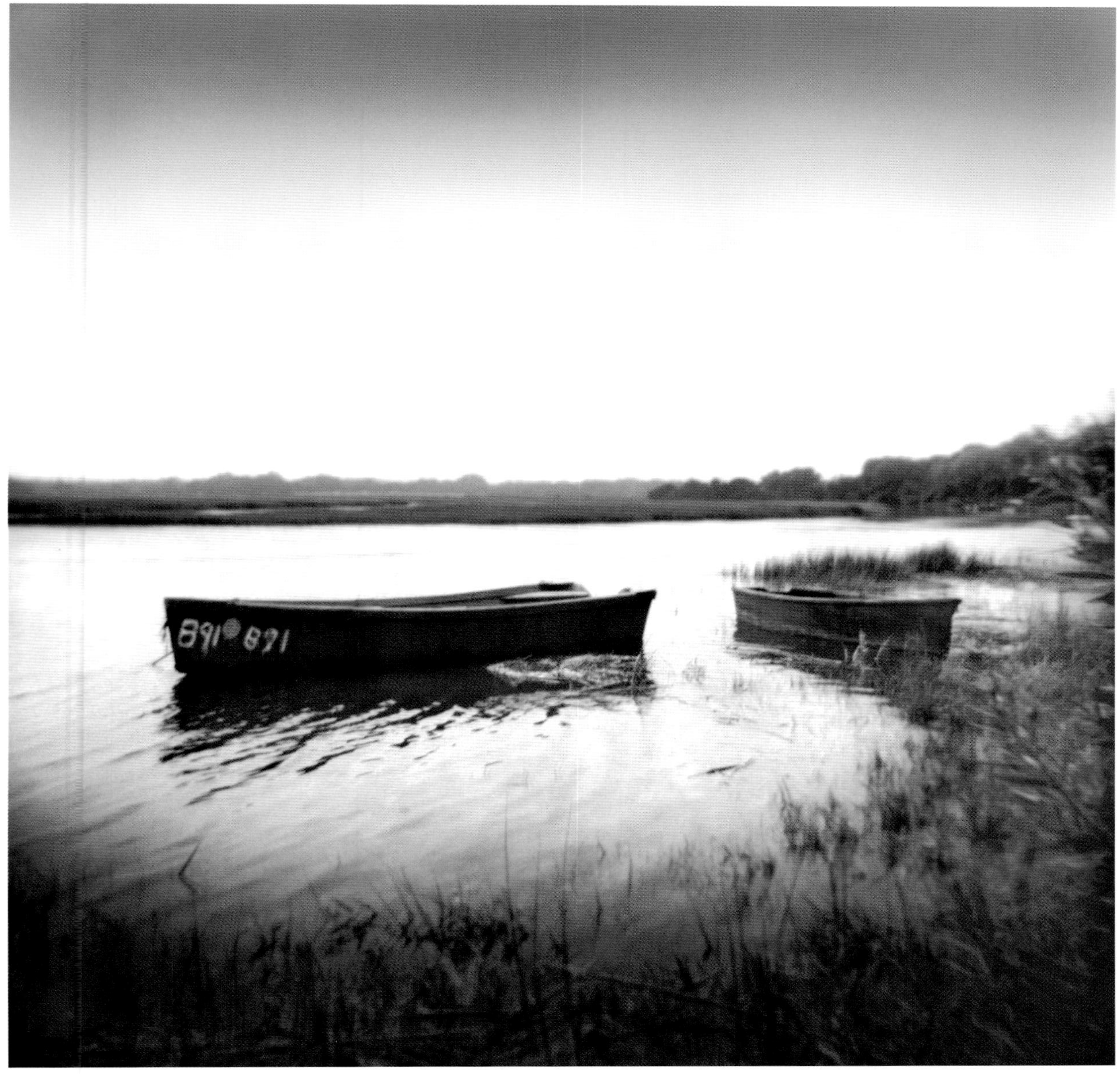
B91 891

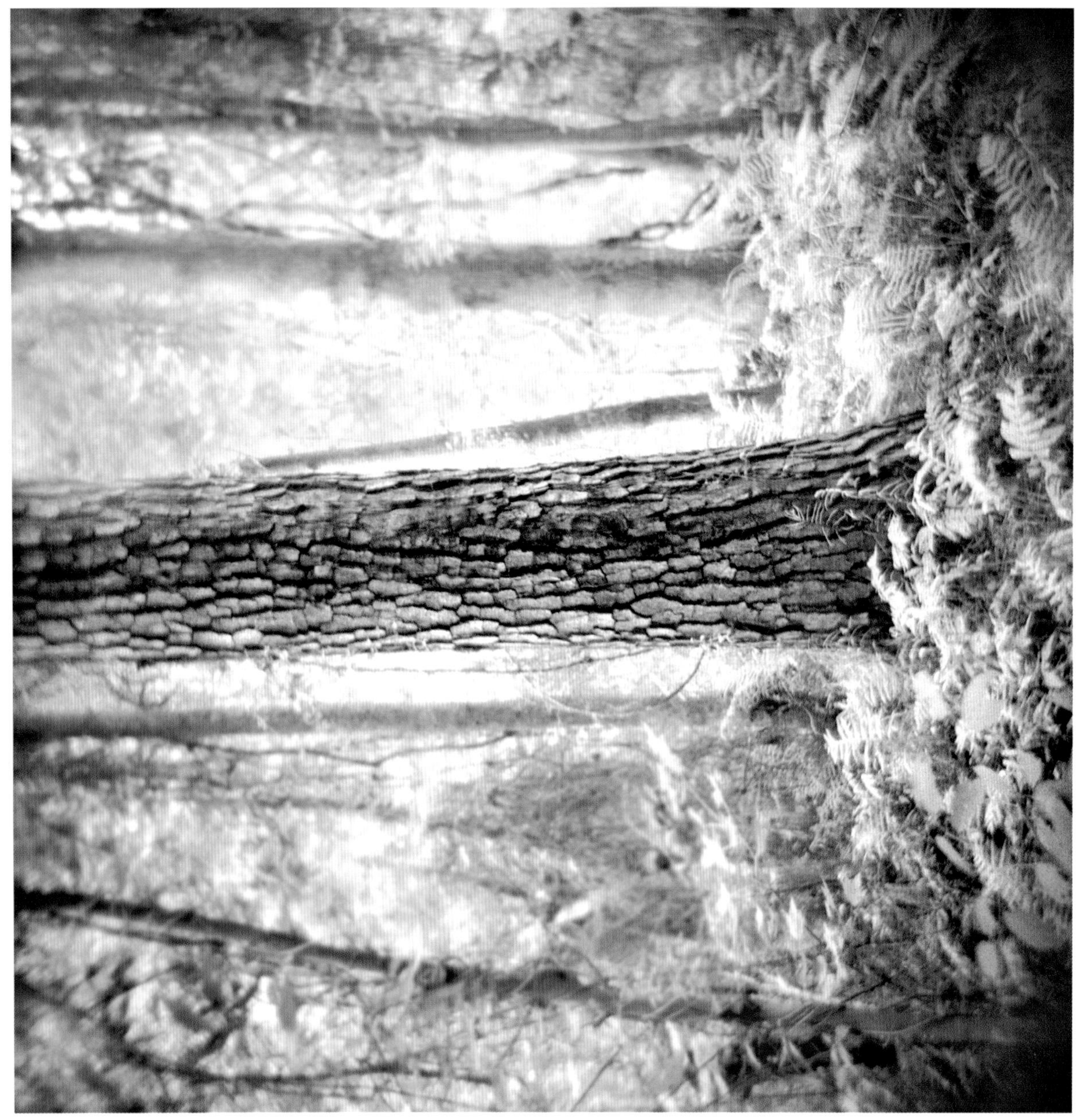

Sweetgrass for hand-sewn baskets grows alongside causeways; tides channel through concrete pipes instead of Spartina grass and oyster banks. Live oaks stand like protected masts adrift in seas of manicured lawns and putting greens. Magnolia, dogwood, long-leaf pine and cypress trees fight for relevance among new homes, new roads and expanding church parking lots.

It isn't natural, the pace of this race to subdivide, post and guard. The Lowcountry used to be a slow country. Its uniqueness depended on a certain pace, a lilt to life. Dogs could nap on dirt roads; grits weren't instant; conversations weren't measured in cell phone minutes. Killing time was never wasting time.

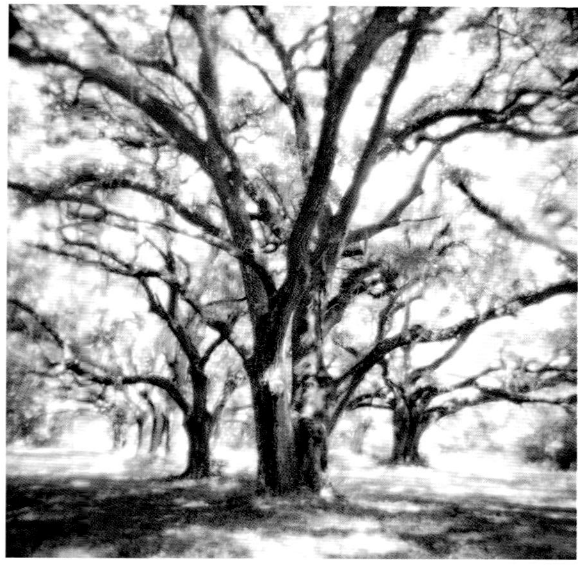
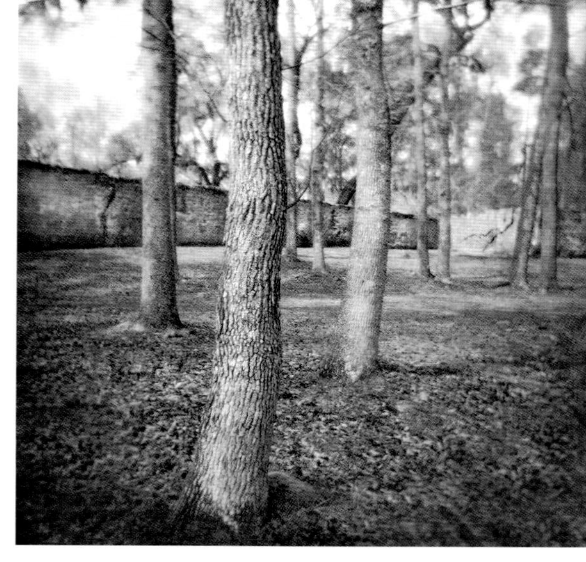
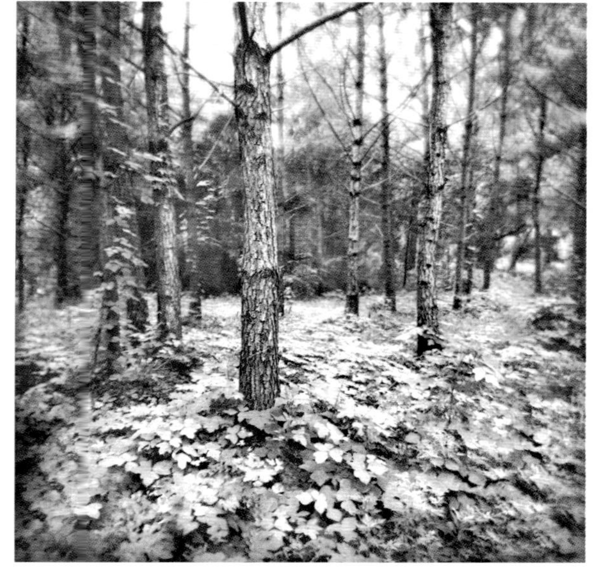
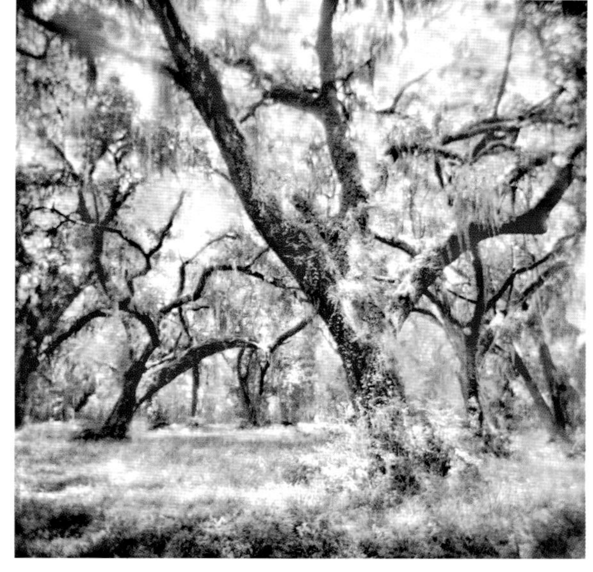

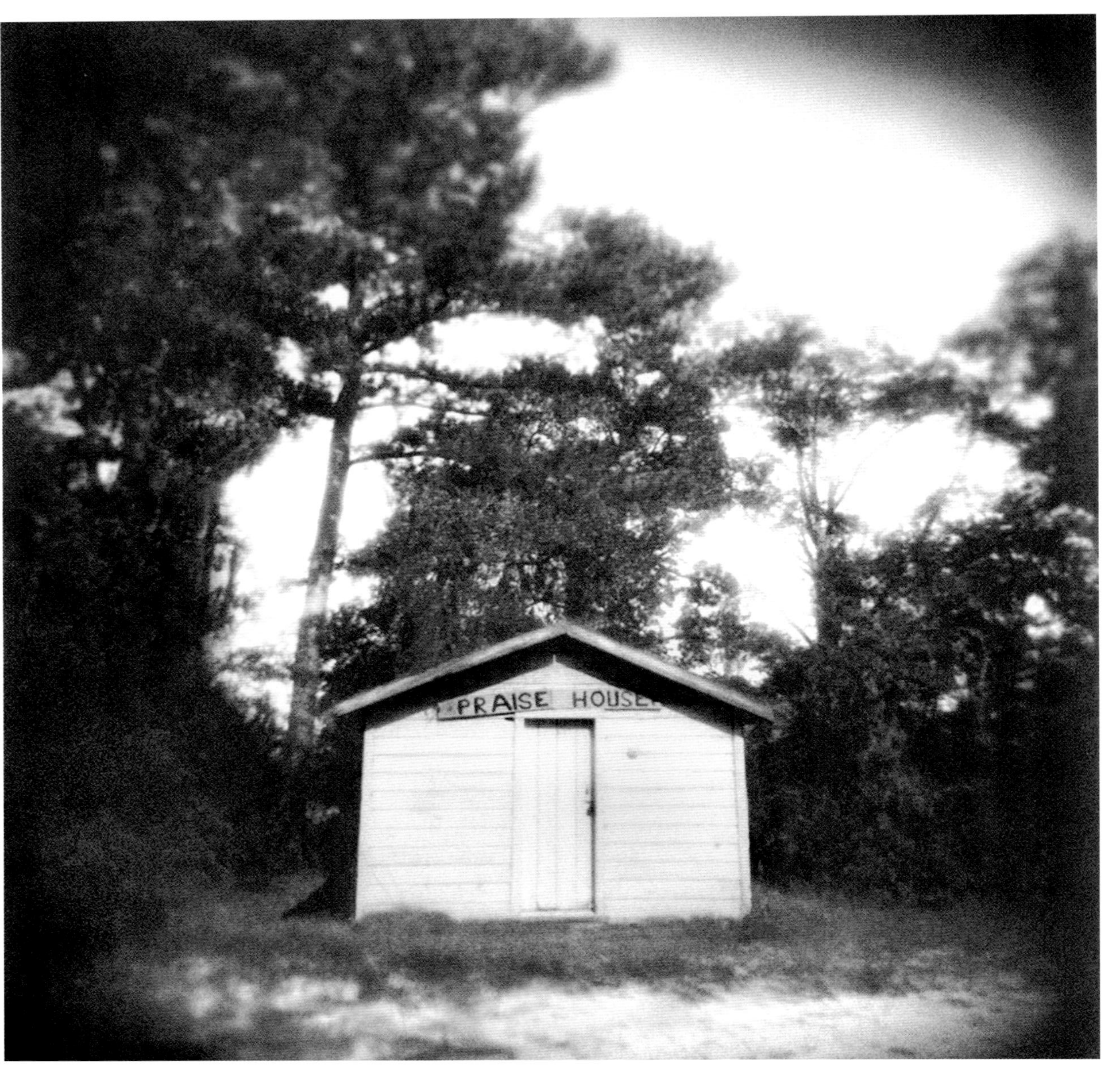
PRAISE HOUSE

New arrivals spend time golfing, shopping, driving, building. Everything new and fast is named for something old and slow: Live Oak Loop, Sweetgrass Plaza, River's Edge and Heron's Way. It isn't surprising. Just ask the Gullah people who lived here before the top ten lists in magazines, and before bicycle paths appeared in gated communities. They have experience in watching and waiting. But in the end, the Lowcountry can't be saved in schools or preserved in museums. To "protect" implies more fragility than the truth of this barrier-strong, bug-swarmed, heat-baked place. "Preserve" is a passive euphemism; juicy berries turned to sticky jam. The verbs we use to declare our intent need to evolve – "crack the teeth," as the Gullah say, and shout, advocate, celebrate, treasure, teach and witness. That's more like it.

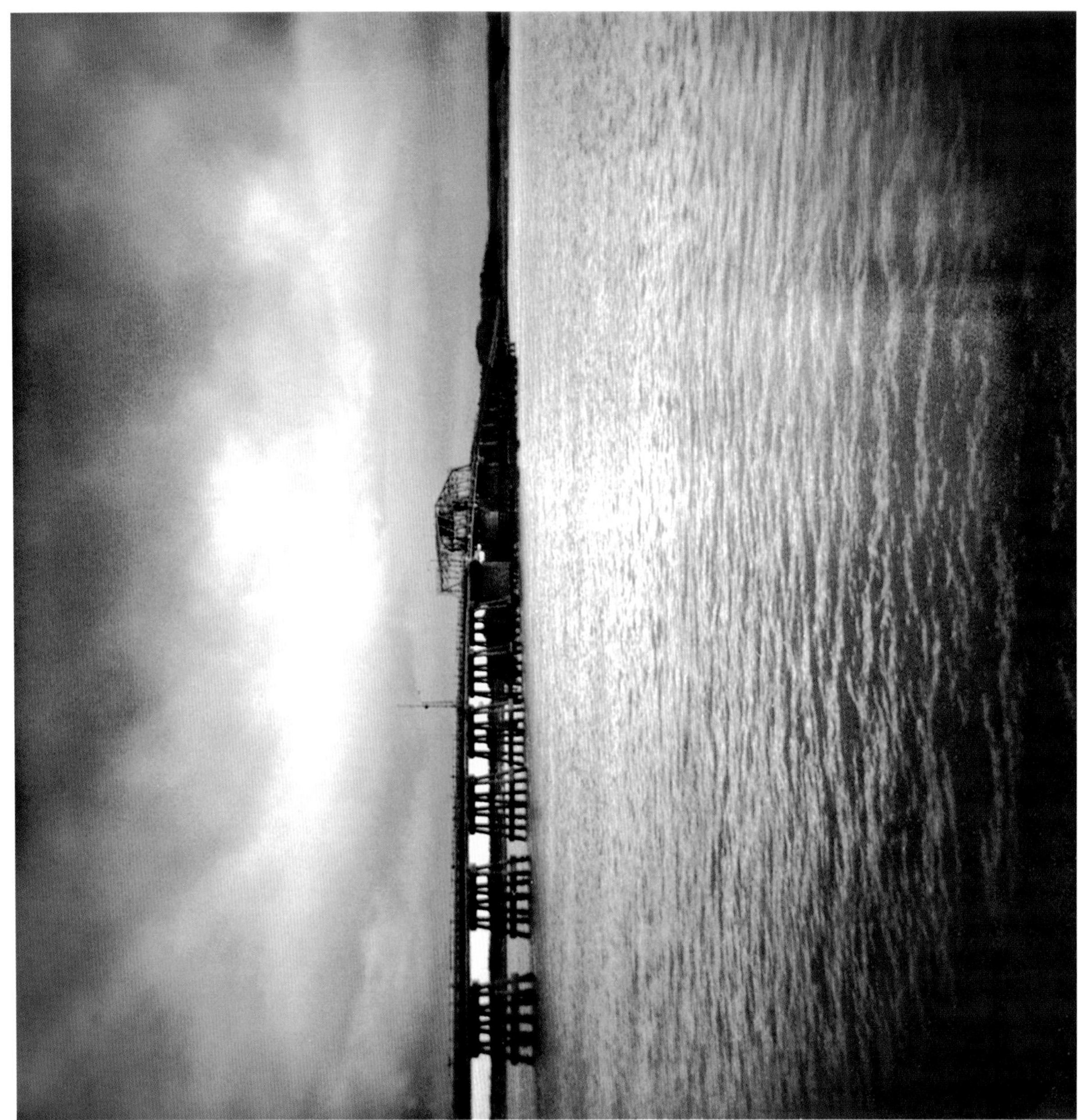

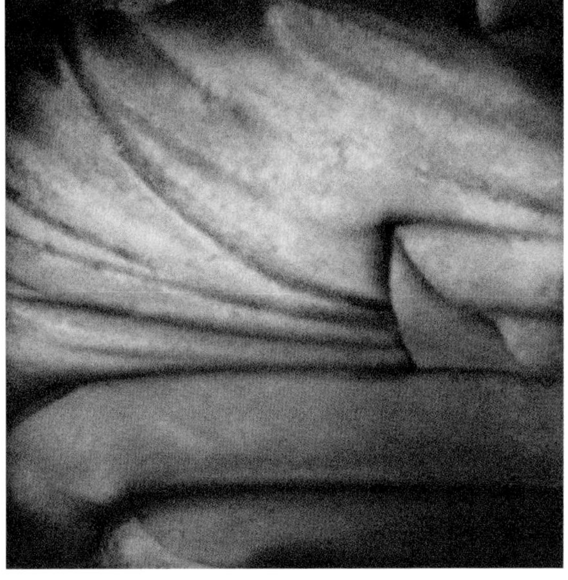

No moat can keep others out; no drawbridge will justify first-come, first-served. Developers are delighted. Realtors have buyers. Churches have congregations. Teachers have students. Farmers have customers. Hospitals have patients. In the parlance of economic development, the Lowcountry is at the "threshold of viability."

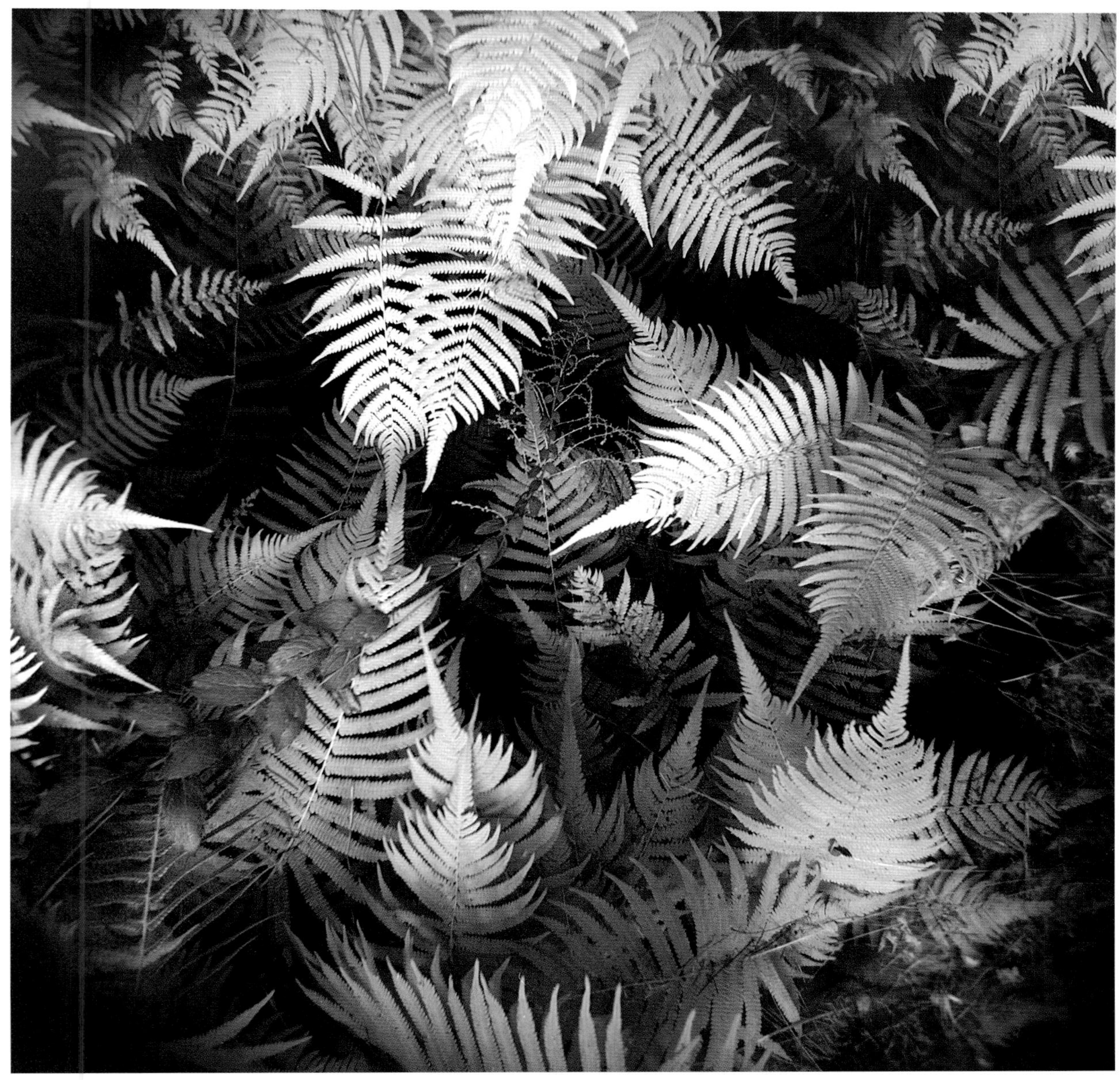

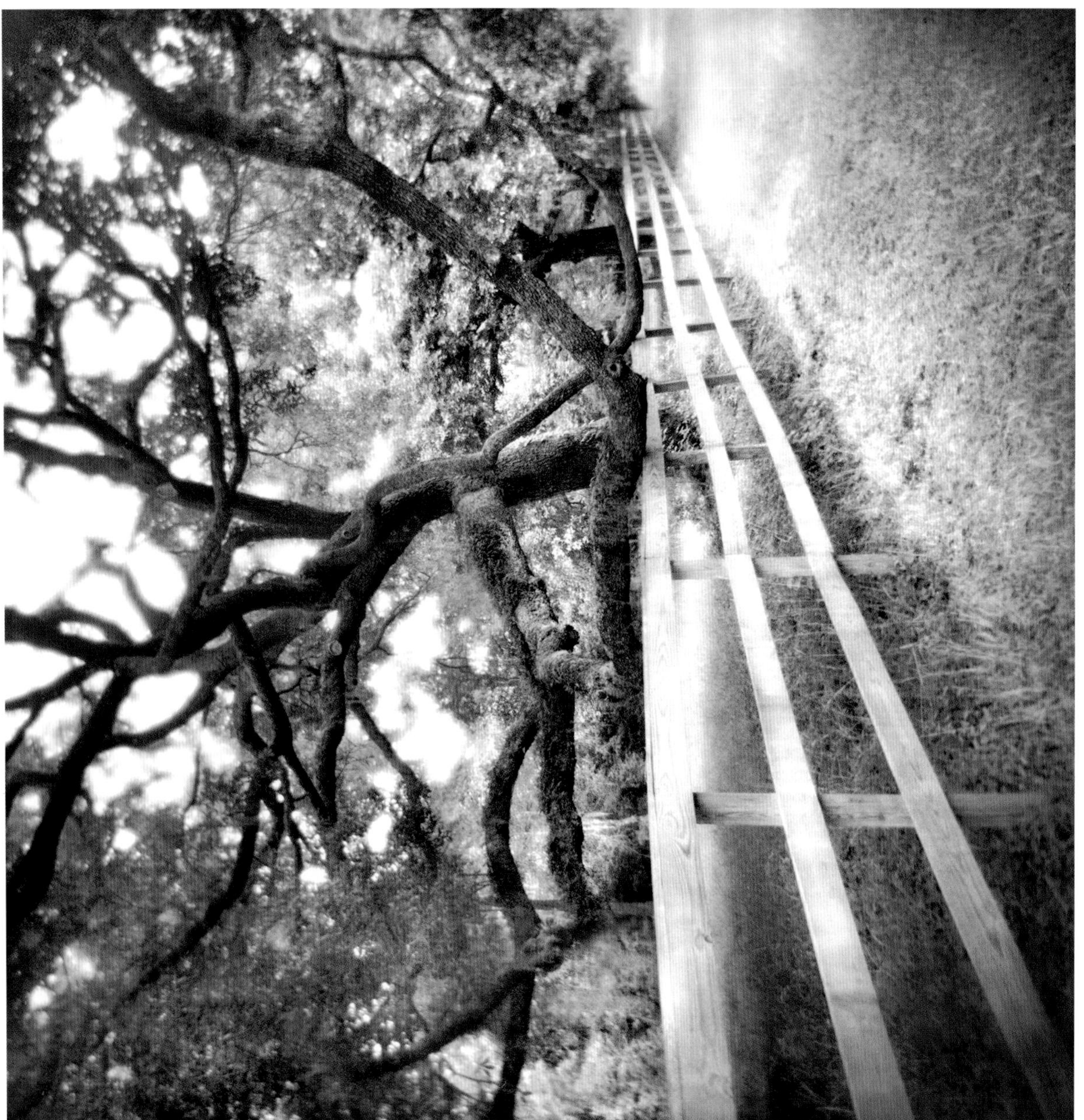

To national retail chains, this means opportunity – the Lowcountry is full of affluent baby boomers retiring with pension plans. There are capital gains to reinvest and water, fish, golf and the weather to enjoy. Whether these "come yahs" become one with this place depends on a richer vocabulary, a deeper understanding.

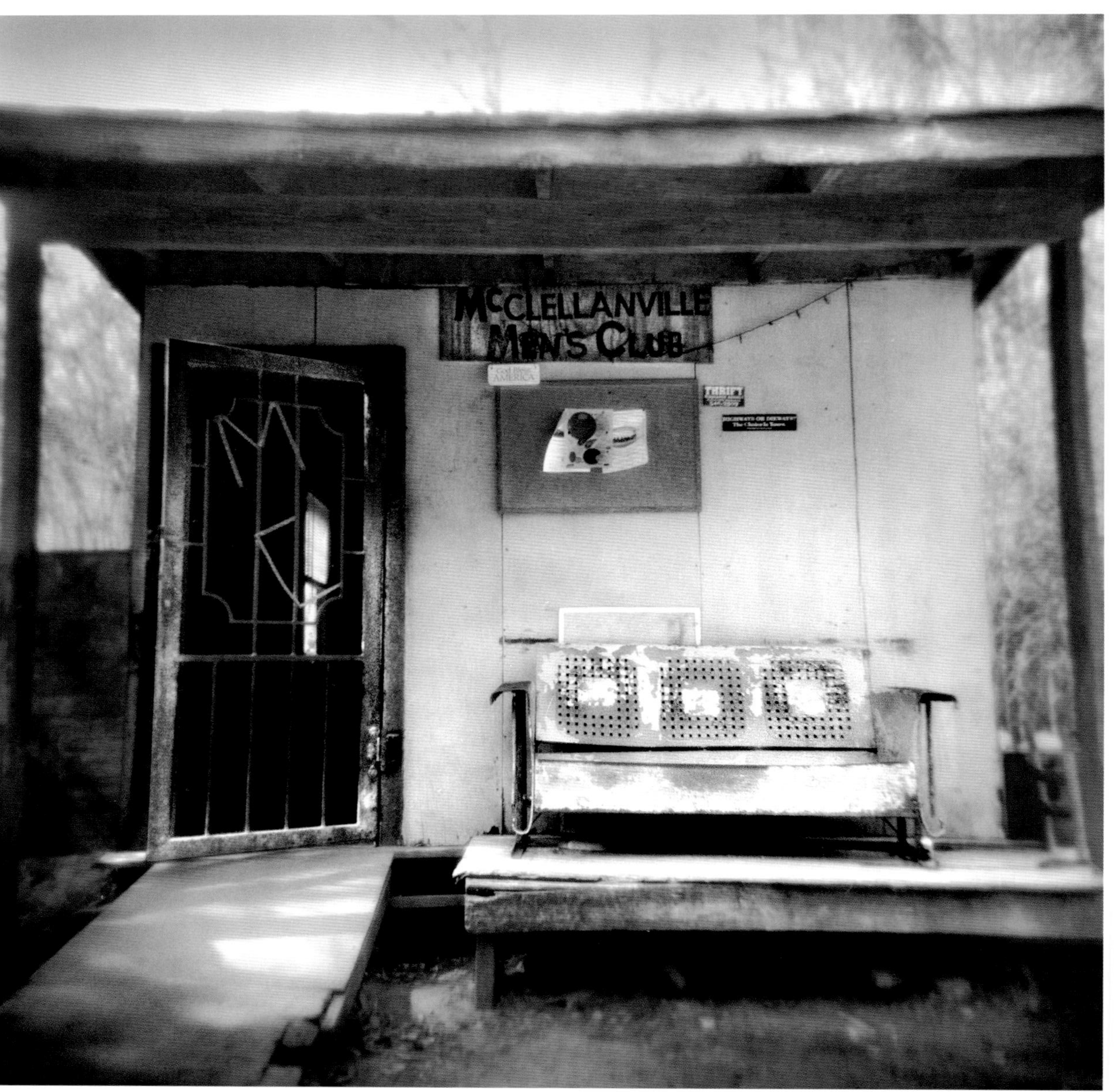
McCLELLANVILLE
MEN'S CLUB
AMERICA
THRIFT

It is freely offered, this potential
for a gentle dance
between the old and new.

Every swath of moon-drained marsh is chaperone. The music is morning bird song and spirituals. The steps are in the details of every iron entrance gate. The style is in the delicate pattern of pale camellia blossoms, the bounce in azaleas wild with fuchsia. The rhythm blows through the Spanish moss; the syncopation is the shifting tides. We have to follow before we can lead, and there is much to learn.

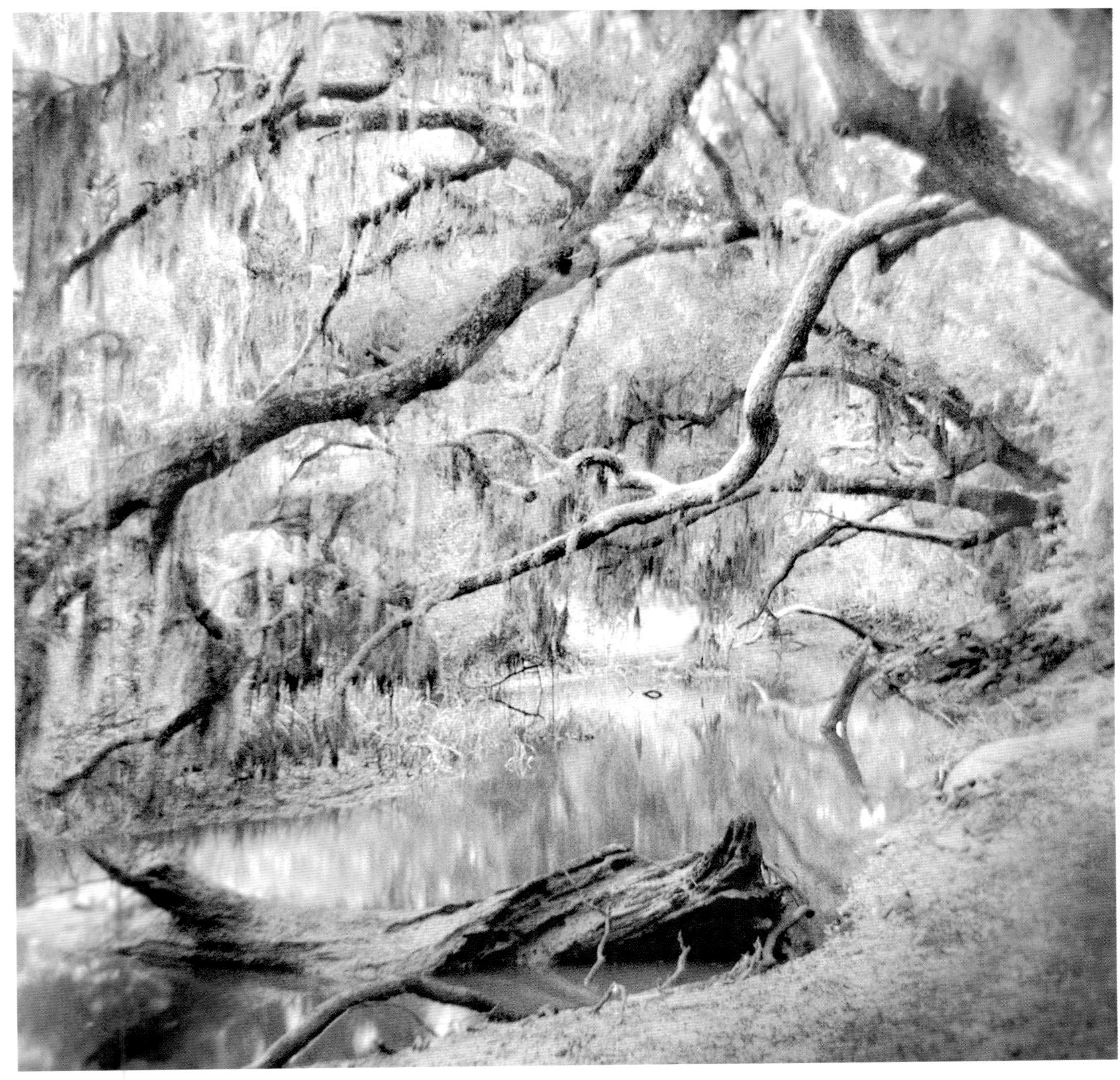

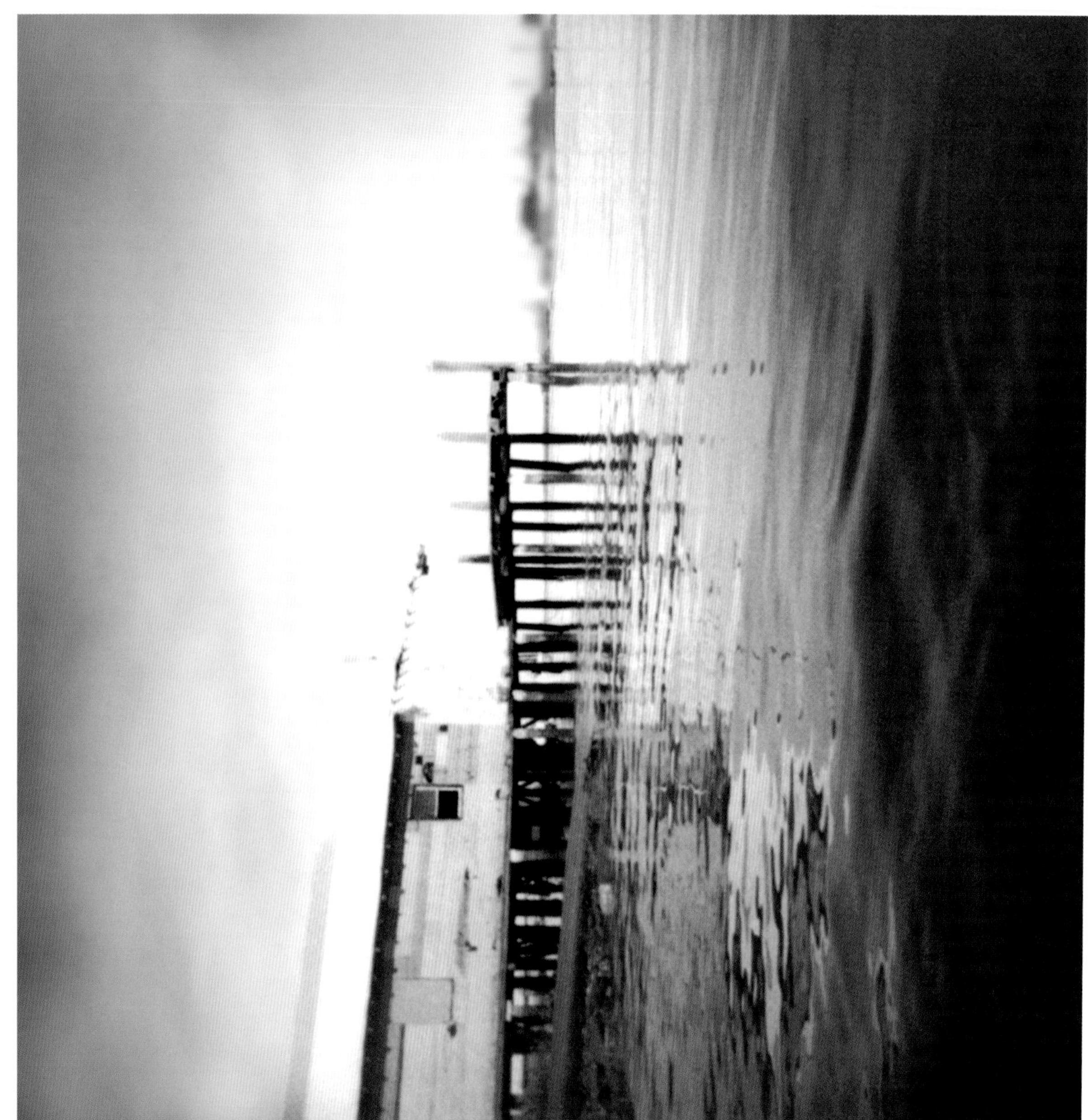

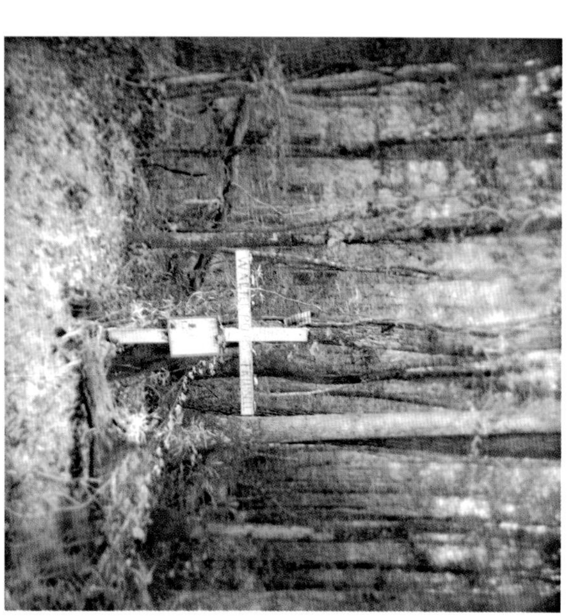

There are historical markers along roads that ask us to wander into woods to find where battles raged and churches burned. There are landings that look out on rivers with names said out loud far from how they read on maps. There are stories behind every tipped-over headstone, souls "gone home," beloved still.

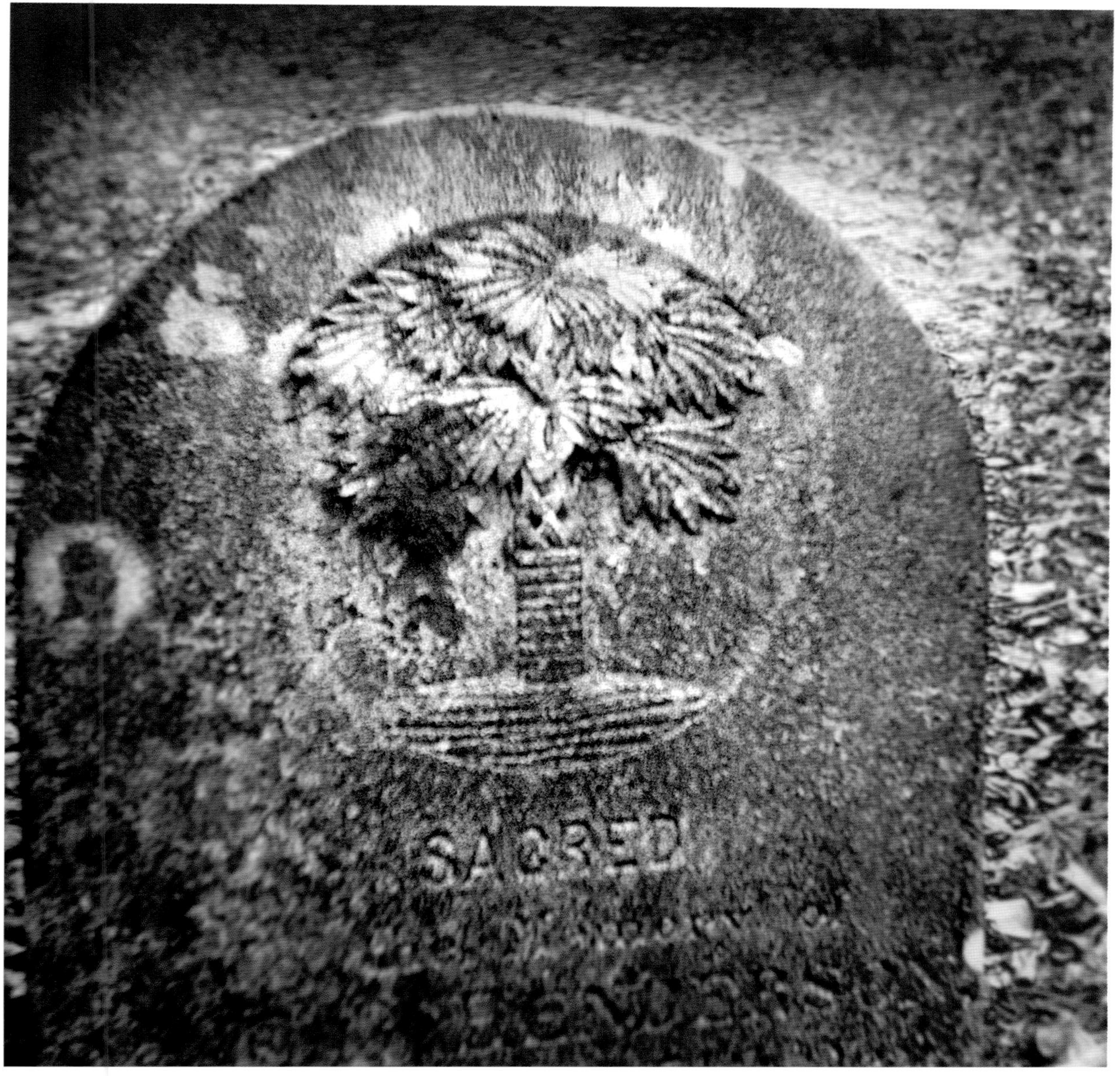
SACRED

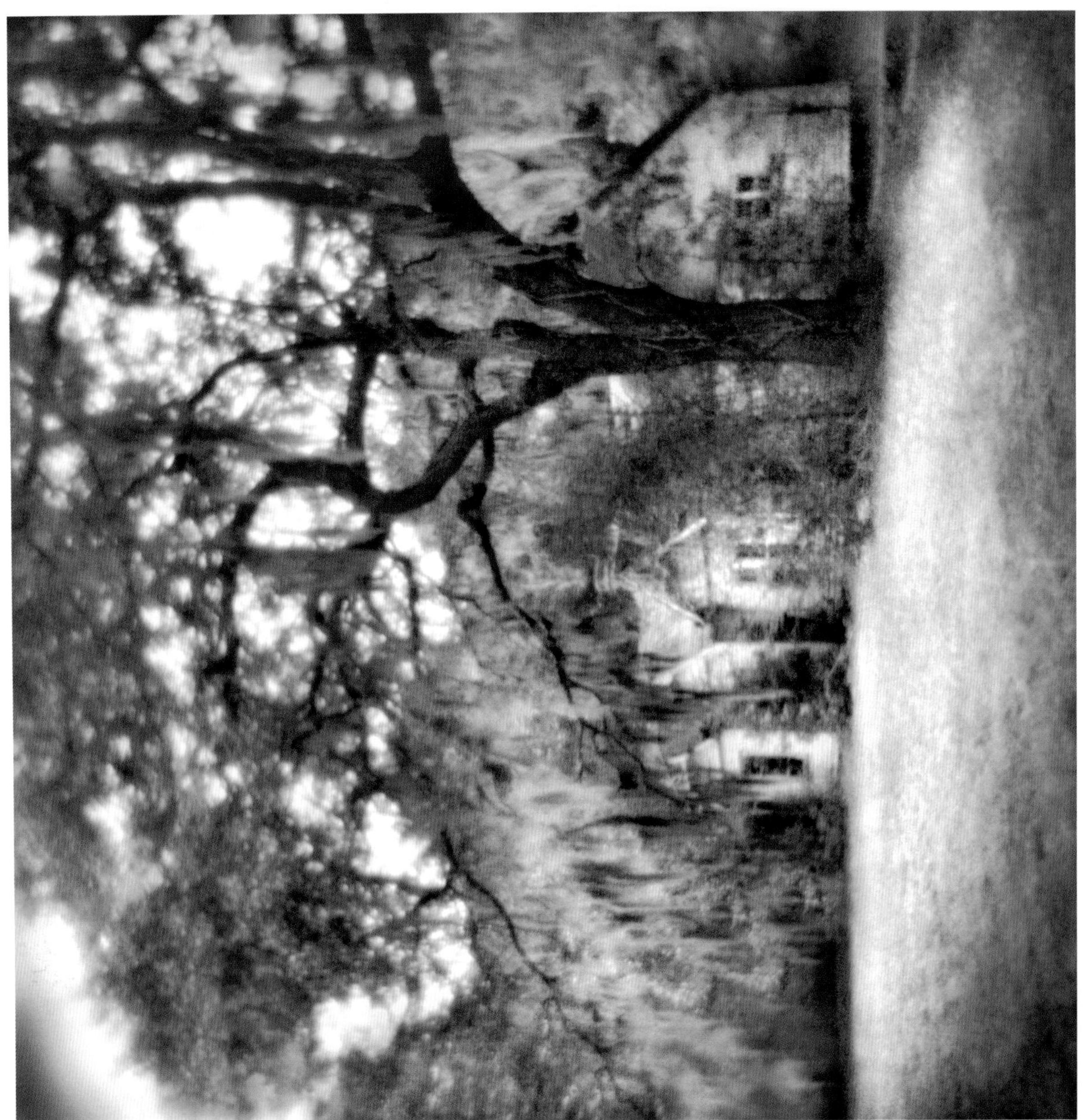

There are back roads that connect extended families down "JB Lane" and "Ida's Path." There are generations of boiled peanuts in Garden's Corner, fried crab cakes in Walterboro and Frogmore stew and shrimp burgers on St. Helena Island. Grandmothers save chicken necks and string to lure blue crabs through the pluff mud. On the front porches of restored mansions, Pawleys Island hammocks stretch languidly, inviting. In the spring, silver-haired ladies tell the secrets of their gardens for charities and compliments. Candidates kiss babies at autumn oyster roasts and judge talent competitions at summer festivals. Dolphins follow shrimp boats through the creeks to smelly docks and beat-up trucks. Middle school students study the story of Robert Smalls and the Port Royal Experiment. The department of motor vehicles is closed for Confederate Memorial Day.

Backyard farmers park pickups full of melons and collard greens under the shade of emancipation oaks. Latinos ease tomatoes from their vines where slaves once gathered cotton.

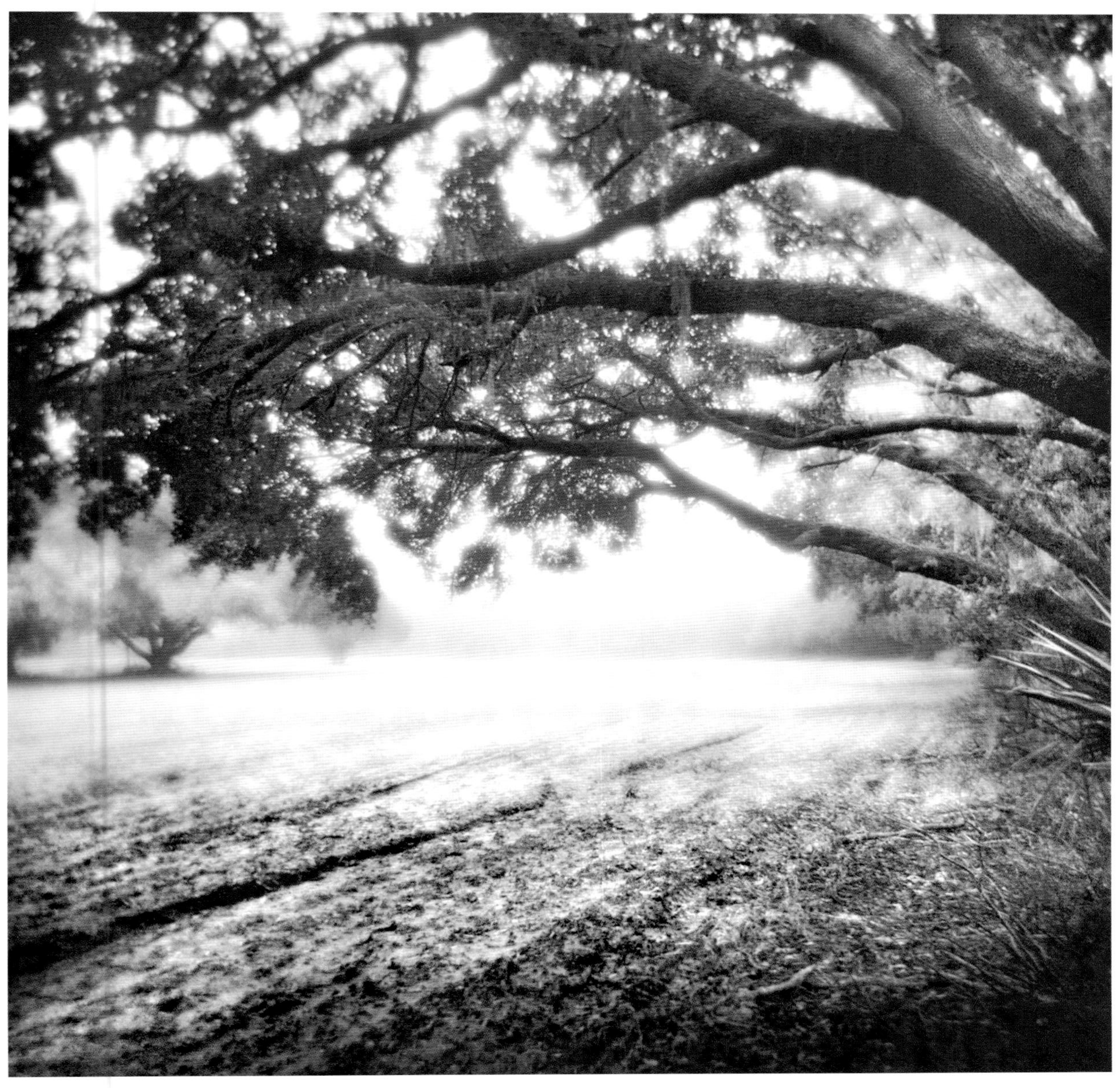

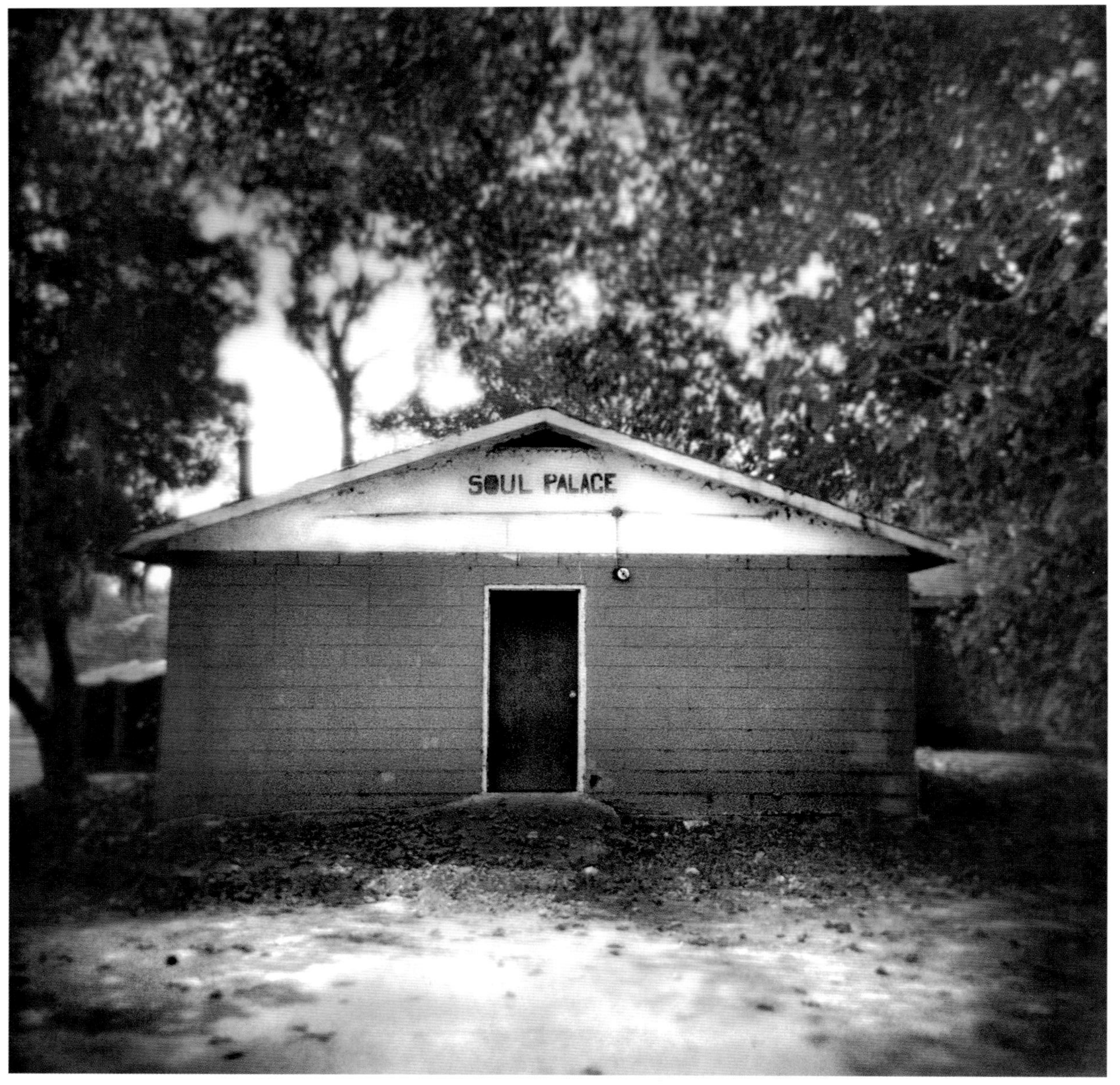
SOUL PALACE

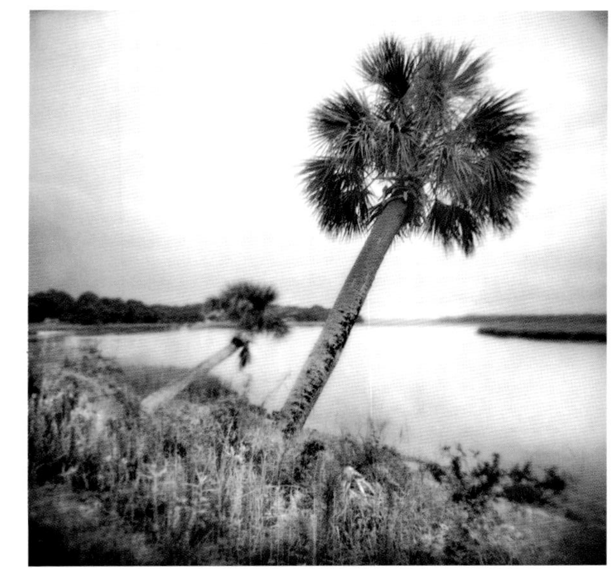

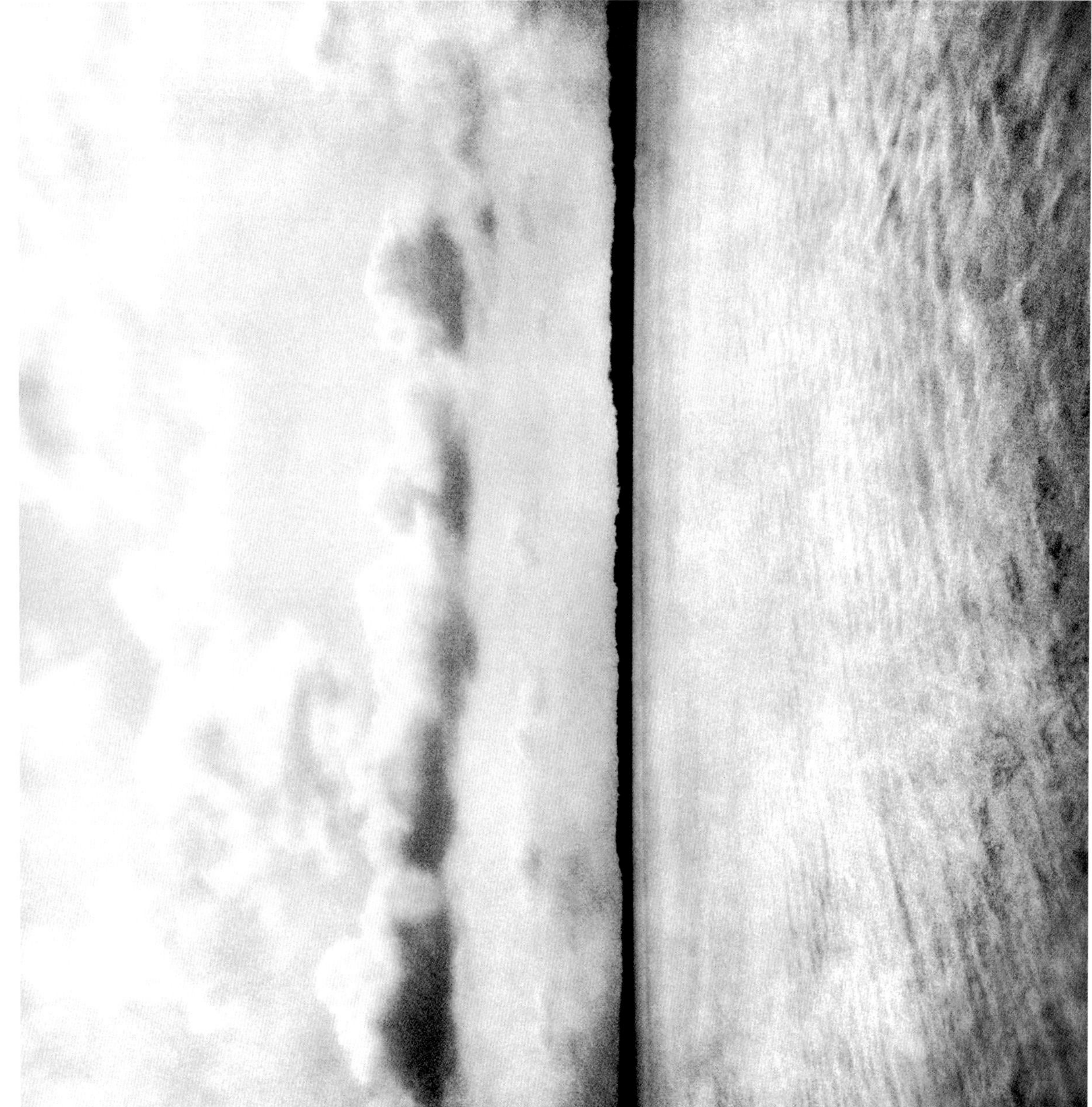

It is a tangled and complicated beauty here,
a meandering and melancholy story.

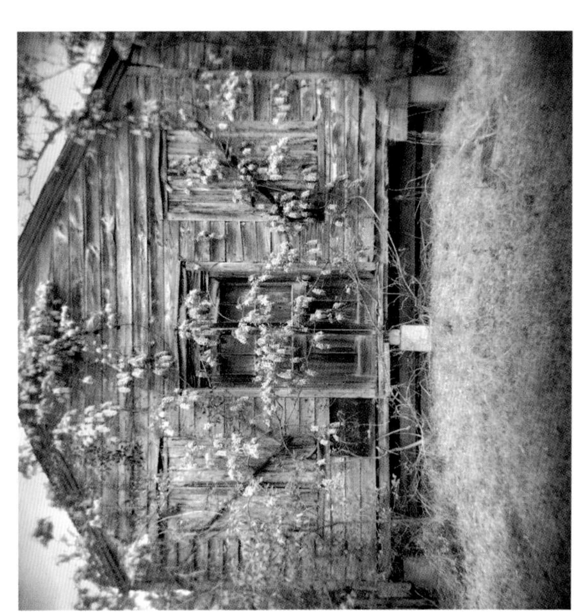

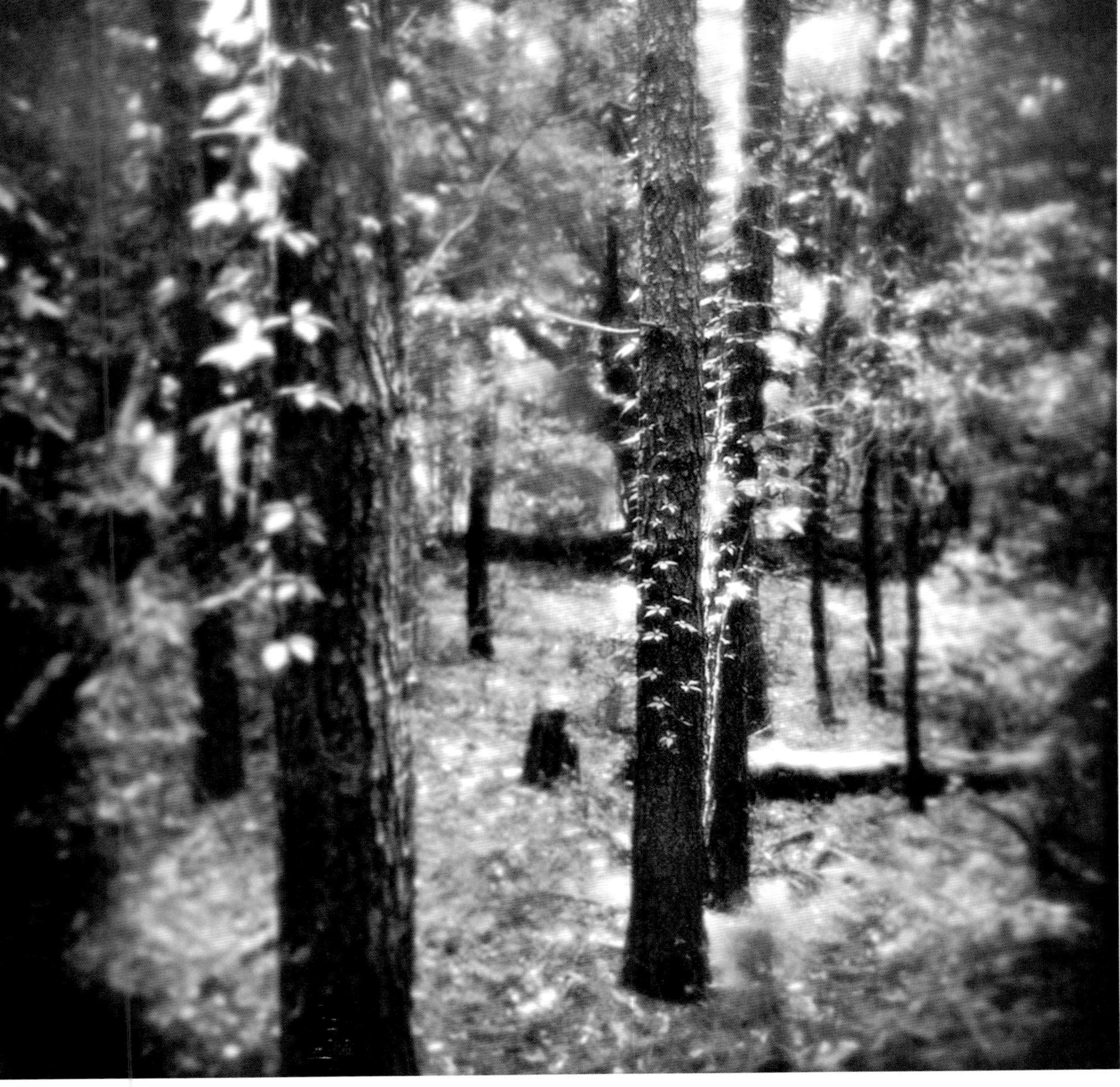

If you are lucky enough to be from
here, they are the reason you stay.

If you have only just arrived, the images are what you tried to tell your friends back home about this place. They are what you felt when you closed your eyes that first night and pictured the memories you will create here.

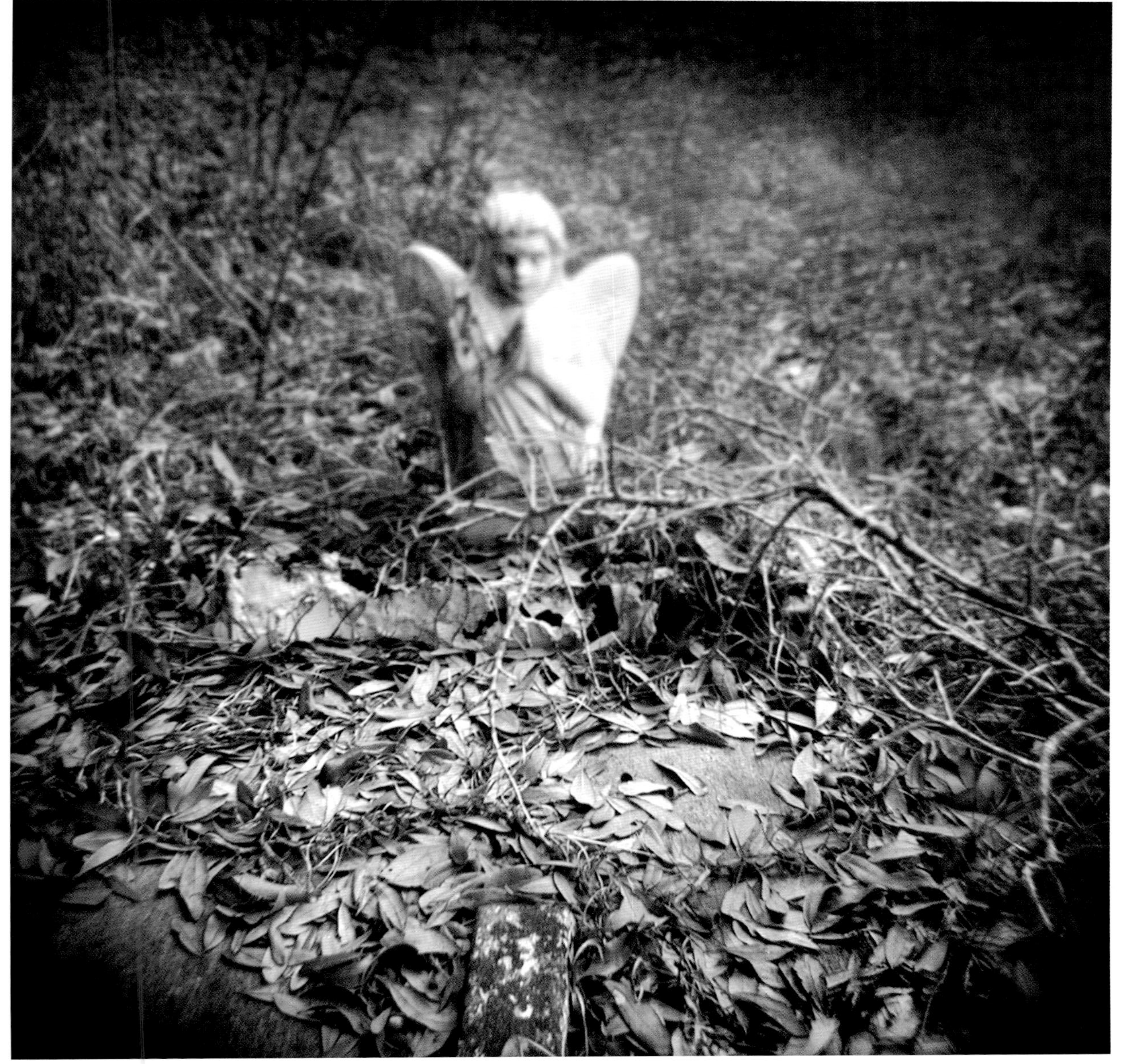

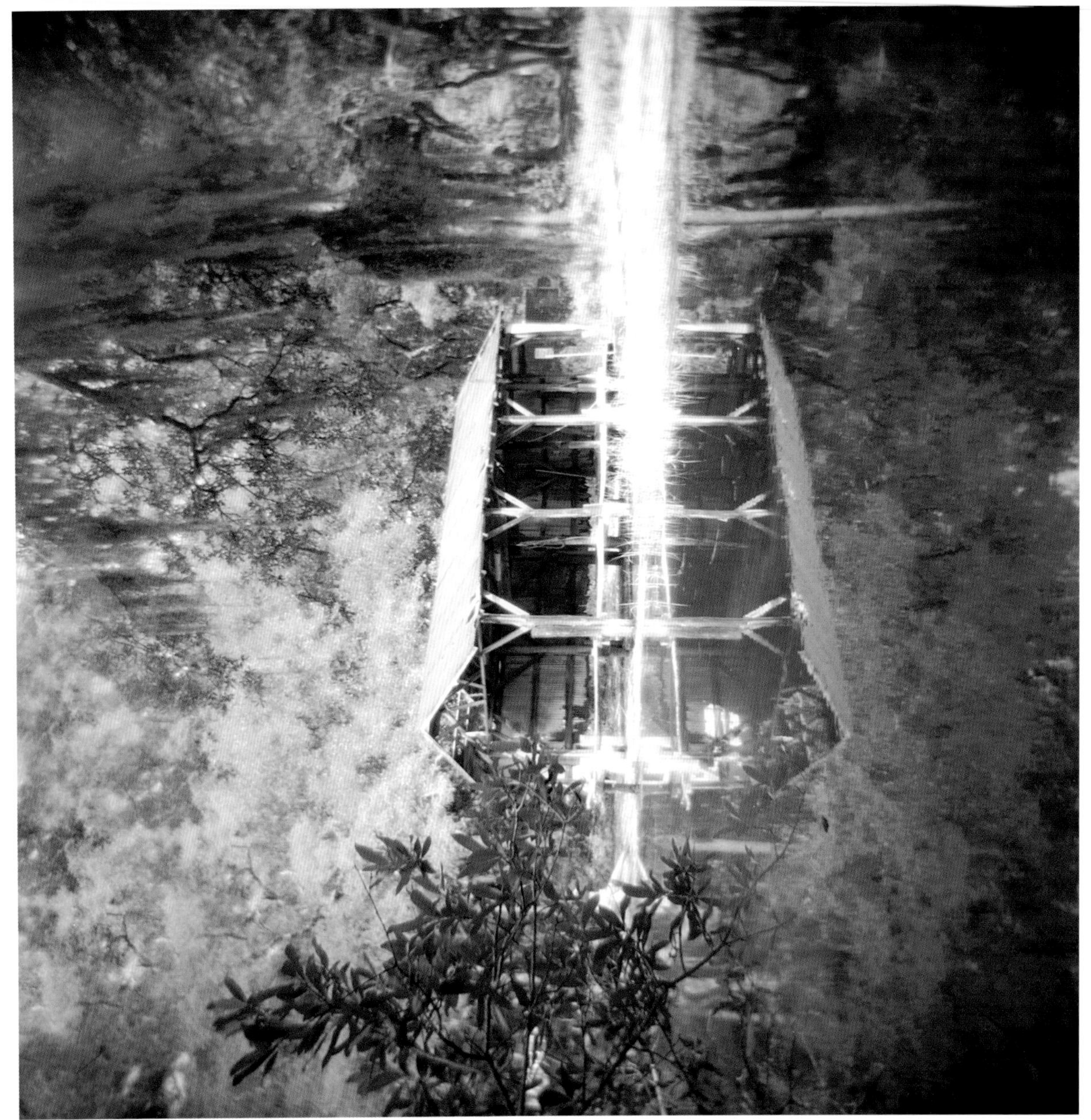

These are the woods and the creeks and the buildings you want to show your grandchildren. For now, at least, you can. The photographs were taken from places accessible to anyone willing to walk, wait and listen to the Lowcountry. These are the places still open and shared and public; gifts passed down from those before us. In them is the grace of times past – for even in struggle, injustice and change, there is grace.

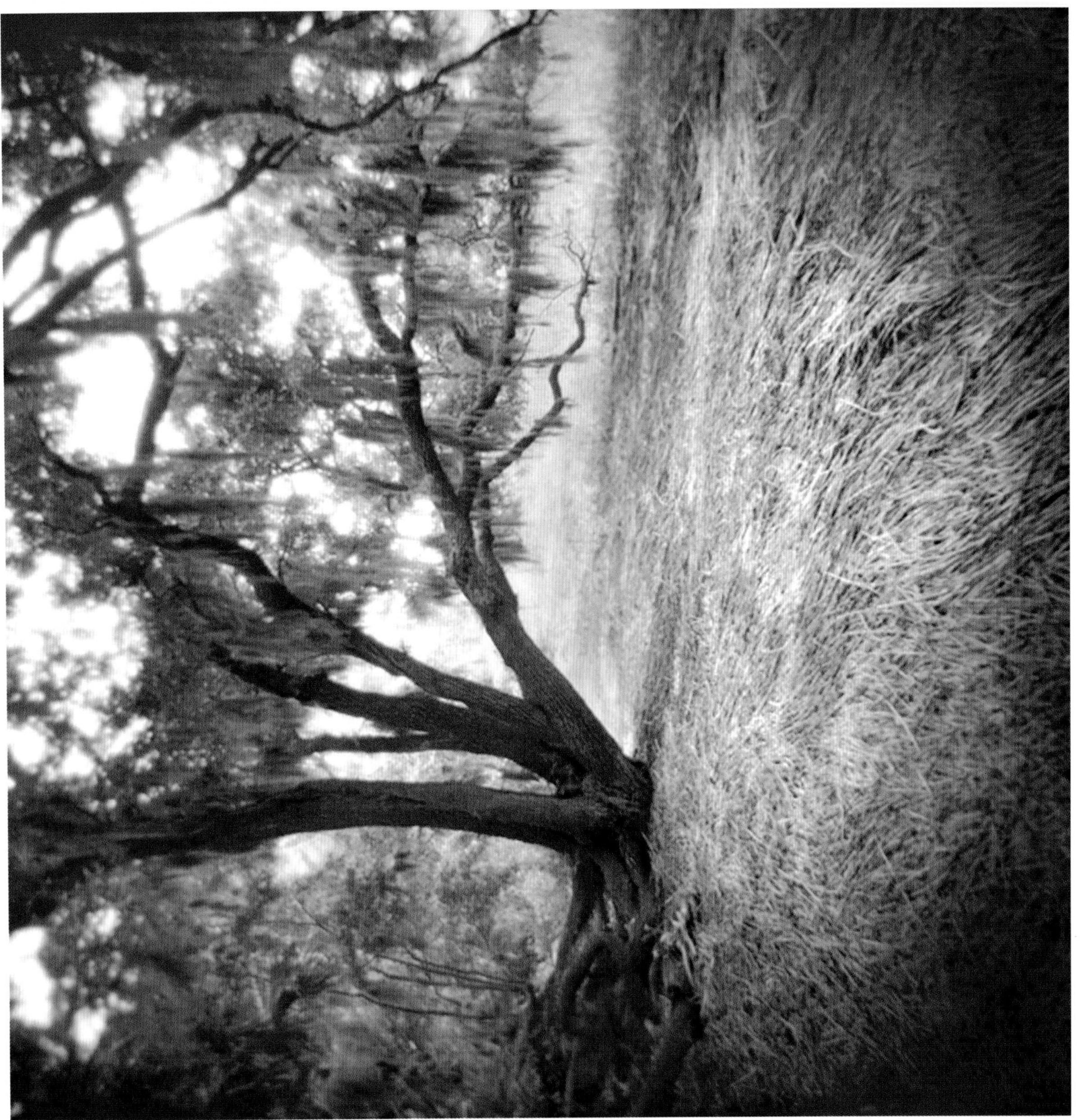

Even in progress, there is pause.

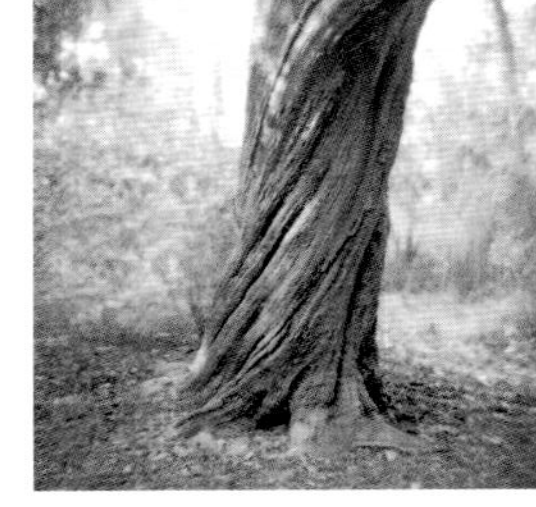

ABOUT THE WORK

Transfer of Grace represents places, moods and moments found along the back roads and left-alone islands of the South Carolina Lowcountry. The glamorous golf courses and gated developments have their own aesthetic – but photographer Gary Geboy is drawn to the timeless essence of the land. In the short time he has lived among them, he has come to see the live oaks, creaky wrought-iron gates and reed-matted creeks not as colorful backdrop but as central character.

To reveal this character, he strips each scene of color. What's left is the positive and negative space, the enduring forms underpinning the beauty. In black and white, humidity is palpable, the seasons connected. The colors of Lowcountry landscape are subtle, reflections more than revelations, formed along a continuum from the ephemeral to the grounded. The graceful herons and swinging hammocks are warm, cotton white. The wrought-iron gates and wooden joggling boards are the blackest green. The shrimp and the nets that catch them are a fleshy opalescence. The tabby ruins of chapels of ease are the cream of oysters and sand. The headstones under live oak trees are gray with age – the meeting place of black and white blended in time and tone. The Spanish moss is the same shadow gray, dripping down like a shroud to shelter the earth from the thick, white heat of the sky.

The images in *Transfer of Grace* were created over the space of eighteen months and in the light of five different Lowcountry counties. Every season and every hour of the day is represented, as fluid as the waters that connect them. For Geboy, the process was an exploration, not in the pursuit of discovery but of character. In every abandoned building, he saw a human story; in every lovingly planted live oak, a legacy. The photos are the mysteries and the questions that lingered after every foray into the almost forgotten.

Each image is an impression, purposefully void of detail so that the observer is free to interpret – some hint at memories and lifestyles replaced or abandoned in pursuit of progress. They may trigger universal feelings about places and traditions fading, or already lost. The pages do not attempt to illustrate or document. They are the why, not the what. There are no captions; each image is universal and personal. But the photographs can be no more than metaphors for a state of being – a way of transferring grace along with loss.

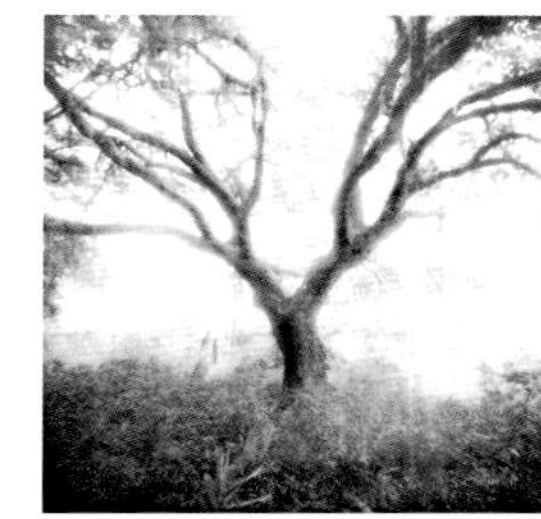

ABOUT THE PUBLISHER

Joggling boards are responsible for many an unlikely pairing in South Carolina – strategically positioned as they are on the elegant front porches of Charleston. The long wooden plank suspended between two rocker springs practically forces those who sit on either end to wind up side by side. And so it was for the two founders of Joggling Board Press. Susan Kammeraad-Campbell was from the North; Douglas W. Bostick as Southern as they come. They found in each other an ideal counterpart to bounce around ideas – in this case, for novel approaches to publishing high-quality niche books of regional interest.

Kammeraad-Campbell was already a published author; her book, *Doc: The Story of Dennis Littky and his Fight for a Better School,* was made into an NBC movie called *A Town Torn Apart.* Bostick had spent two decades actively collecting and piecing together histories of the South and publishing them in historical journals and magazines. More than three years and ten books later, the decidedly unconventional Joggling Board Press has printed its own path. The region's rich culture is offered to all those interested; the most authentic of its histories are shared from the learned to the eager. Meetings often take place over meals, work happens where and when it works best, and what results is as creative as it is thorough.

Joggling boards are long, capable of seating many at a time. Joggling Board Press contributors join Kammeraad-Campbell and Bostick when their expertise is needed – from scholarly review to graphic design. For *Transfer of Grace*, Courtney Gunter worked with the partners and the photographer to design the cover and the layout. Her sense of pacing, balance, texture and color transforms a collection of emotional images into a visual poem.

PRODUCTION NOTES

The production of an art book of museum quality requires attention to detail, from the opacity of the paper and how it takes up ink to the selection of inks and print process. *Transfer of Grace* is printed on Japanese/Korean 150 gsm matte, a double-coated stock that takes up ink well. Two PMS colors – Black and Warm Gray 11 – were laid down using a duotone process. Cover fonts are Minion and DIN; the inside font is Minion; bindery is casebound and Smythe sewn. The book was printed in Hong Kong by Regal Press, a company that takes meticulous care with each project it produces.